Extensible Stylesheet Language (XSL) Version 1.0

WD-xsl-19981216

World Wide Web Consortium Working Draft 16-December-1998

Extensible Stylesheet Language (XSL) Version 1.0

WD-xsl-19981216

World Wide Web Consortium Working Draft 16-December-1998

toExcel

New York   San Jose   Lincoln   Shanghai

Extensible Stylesheet Language (XSL) Version 1.0

WD-xsl-19981216

World Wide Web Consortium Working Draft 16-December-1998

Open Documents Standards Library
Published by toExcel
an imprint of iUniverse.com, Inc.

For information address:
iUniverse.com, Inc.
620 North 48th Street
Suite 201
Lincoln, NE 68504-3467
www.iUniverse.com

ISBN: 1-58348-257-1

LCCN: 99-63364

Printed in the United States of America

0 9 8 7 6 5 4 3 2 1

Contents at a Glance

Contents

xii   Extensible Stylesheet Language (XSL)

Abstract

XSL is a language for expressing stylesheets. It consists of two parts:

1. a language for transforming XML documents, and
2. an XML vocabulary for specifying formatting semantics.

An XSL stylesheet specifies the presentation of a class of XML documents by describing how an instance of the class is transformed into an XML document that uses the formatting vocabulary.

Version Information

This version:

```
http://www.w3.org/TR/1998/WD-xsl-19981216
http://www.w3.org/TR/1998/WD-xsl-19981216.xml
http://www.w3.org/TR/1998/WD-xsl-19981216.html
http://www.w3.org/TR/1998/WD-xsl-19981216.pdf
```

Latest version:

```
http://www.w3.org/TR/WD-xsl
```

Previous versions:

```
http://www.w3.org/TR/1998/WD-xsl-19980818
```

Editors:

James Clark (jjc@jclark.com) [Tree Construction]

Stephen Deach, Adobe (sdeach@adobe.com) [Formatting Objects]

Status of this document

This is a W3C Working Draft for review by W3C members and other interested parties. This adds additional functionality to what was described in the previous draft, however the basic design of the previous draft remains unchanged. It is a draft document and may be updated, replaced, or obsoleted by other documents at any time. The XSL Working Group will not allow early implementation to constrain its ability to make changes to this specification prior to final release. It is inappropriate to use W3C Working Drafts as reference material or to cite them as other than "work in progress". A list of current W3C working drafts can be found at http://www.w3.org/TR.

Comments may be sent to xsl-editors@w3.org. Public discussion of XSL takes place on the XSL-List mailing list.

DOCUMENT NOTICE

Chapter 1

Overview

XSL is a language for expressing stylesheets. Each stylesheet describes rules for presenting a class of XML source documents. There are two parts to the presentation process. First, the result tree is constructed from the source tree. Second, the result tree is interpreted to produce formatted output on a display, on paper, in speech or onto other media.

The first part, constructing the result tree, is achieved by associating patterns with templates. A pattern is matched against elements in the source tree. A template is instantiated to create part of the result tree. The result tree is separate from the source tree. The structure of the result tree can be completely different from the structure of the source tree. In constructing the result tree, the source tree can be filtered and reordered, and arbitrary structure can be added.

The second part, formatting, is achieved by using the formatting vocabulary specified in this document to construct the result tree. Formally, this vocabulary is an XML namespace. Each element type in the vocabulary corresponds to a formatting object class. A formatting object class represents a particular kind of formatting behavior. For example, the block formatting object class represents the breaking of the content of a paragraph into lines. Each attribute in the vocabulary corresponds to a formatting property. A formatting object class has a specific set of formatting properties which provide finer control over the behavior of the formatting object class; for example, controlling indenting of lines, spacing between lines, and spacing before and after the collection of lines. A formatting object can have content, and its formatting behavior is applied to its content.

XSL does not require result trees to use the formatting vocabulary and thus can be used for general XML transformations. For example, XSL can be used to transform XML to "well-formed" HTML, that is, XML that uses the element types and attributes defined by HTML.

When the result tree uses the formatting vocabulary, a conforming XSL implementation must be able to interpret the result tree according to the semantics of the formatting vocabulary as defined in this document; it may also be able to externalize the result tree as XML, but it is not required to be able to do so.

This document does not specify how a stylesheet is associated with an XML document. It is recommended that XSL processors support the mechanism described in [W3C XML Stylesheet].

Chapter 2

Tree Construction

2.1 Overview

A stylesheet contains a set of template rules. A template rule has two parts: a pattern which is matched against nodes in the source tree and a template which can be instantiated to form part of the result tree. This allows a stylesheet to be applicable to a wide class of documents that have similar source tree structures.

A template is instantiated for a particular source element to create part of the result tree. A template can contain elements that specify literal result element structure. A template can also contain elements that are instructions for creating result tree fragments. When a template is instantiated, each instruction is executed and replaced by the result tree fragment that it creates. Instructions can select and process descendant elements. Processing a descendant element creates a result tree fragment by finding the applicable template rule and instantiating its template. Note that elements are only processed when they have been selected by the execution of an instruction. The result tree is constructed by finding the template rule for the root node and instantiating its template.

In the process of finding the applicable template rule, more than one template rule may have a pattern that matches a given element. However, only one template rule will be applied. The method for deciding which template rule to apply is described in Section 2.5.1: Conflict Resolution for Template Rules.

XSL uses XML namespaces [W3C XML Names] to distinguish elements that are instructions to the XSL processor from elements that specify literal result tree structure. Instruction elements all belong to the XSL namespace. The examples in this document use a prefix of `xsl:` for elements in the XSL namespace.

An XSL stylesheet contains an `xsl:stylesheet` document element. This element may contain `xsl:template` elements specifying template rules, which will be described later in this document.

The following is an example of a simple XSL stylesheet that constructs a result tree for a sequence of para elements. The result-ns=" fo" attribute indicates that a tree using the formatting object vocabulary is being constructed. The rule for the root node specifies the use of a page sequence formatted with any font with serifs. The para elements become block formatting objects which are set in 10 point type with a 12 point space before each block.

```
<xsl:stylesheet
  xmlns:xsl="http://www.w3.org/TR/WD-xsl"
  xmlns:fo="http://www.w3.org/TR/WD-xsl/FO"
  result-ns="fo">
  <xsl:template match="/">
    <fo:basic-page-sequence font-family="serif">
        <xsl:apply-templates/>
    </fo:basic-page-sequence>
  </xsl:template>

  <xsl:template match="para">
    <fo:block font-size="10pt" space-before="12pt">
      <xsl:apply-templates/>
    </fo:block>
  </xsl:template>
</xsl:stylesheet>
```

The xsl:stylesheet element can also contain elements importing other XSL stylesheets, elements defining macros, elements defining global constants, and elements identifying source attributes as individual element identifiers.

2.2 Stylesheet Structure

A stylesheet is represented by an xsl:stylesheet element in an XML document.

XSL processors must use the XML namespaces mechanism [W3C XML Names] for both source documents and stylesheets. All XSL defined elements, that is those specified in this document with a prefix of xsl:, will only be recognized by the XSL processor if they belong to a namespace with the URI http://www.w3.org/TR/WD-xsl; XSL defined elements are recognized only in the stylesheet not in the source document.

Issue (versioning): Should there be some way for a stylesheet to indicate which version of XSL it conforms to? Can this be done through the URI of the XSL namespace?

The `xsl:stylesheet` element has an optional result-ns attribute; the value must be a namespace prefix. If this attribute is specified, all result elements must belong to the namespace identified by this prefix (the result namespace). If there is a namespace declared as the default namespace, then an empty string may be used as the value to specify that the default namespace is the result namespace. If the result-ns attribute specifies the XSL Formatting Objects namespace, then in addition to constructing the result XML tree, the XSL processor must interpret it according to the semantics defined in this document. The XSL Formatting Objects namespace has the URI http://www.w3.org/TR/WD-xsl/FO. The examples in this document use the fo: prefix for this namespace.

NOTE: If an implementation wishes to use something in the result tree or stylesheet to control the output of a non-XML representation of the result tree, it should use the result namespace. In particular, if it wishes to make use of something in the result tree or stylesheet to indicate that the result tree should be output as HTML that conforms to the HTML 4.0 Recommendation rather than as XML, it should use a result namespace of http://www.w3.org/TR/REC-html40; for example,

```
<xsl:stylesheet
  xmlns:xsl="http://www.w3.org/TR/WD-xsl"
  xmlns="http://www.w3.org/TR/REC-html40"
  result-ns="">

<xsl:template match="/">
  <html>
   <xsl:apply-templates/>
  </html>
</xsl:template>

  . . .

</xsl:stylesheet>
```

The `xsl:stylesheet` element may contain the following types of elements:

1. `xsl:import`
2. `xsl:include`
3. `xsl:id`

4. `xsl:strip-space`

5. `xsl:preserve-space`

6. `xsl:macro`

7. `xsl:attribute-set`

8. `xsl:constant`

9. `xsl:template`

This example shows the structure of a stylesheet. Ellipses (...) indicate where attribute values or content have been omitted. Although this example shows one of each type of allowed element, stylesheets may contain zero or more of each of these elements.

```
<?xml version="1.0"?>
<xsl:stylesheet xmlns:xsl="http://www.w3.org/TR/WD-xsl">
  <xsl:import href="..."/>
  <xsl:include href="..."/>
  <xsl:id attribute="..."/>
  <xsl:strip-space element="..."/>
    <xsl:preserve-space element="..."/>
  <xsl:macro name="...">

    ...

  </xsl:macro>

  <xsl:attribute-set name="...">

    ...

  </xsl:attribute-set>

  <xsl:constant name="..." value="..."/>

  <xsl:template match="...">

    ...
  </xsl:template>
</xsl:stylesheet>
```

The order in which the children of the `xsl:stylesheet` element occur is not significant except for `xsl:import` elements and for error recovery. Users are free to order the elements as they prefer, and stylesheet creation tools need not provide control over the order in which the elements occur.

Issue (media-rule): Should we provide the functionality of CSS's @media rule and if so how?

2.3 Processing Model

Ed. Note: This needs expanding and polishing.

A node is processed to create a result tree fragment. The result tree is constructed by processing the root node. A node is processed by finding all the template rules with patterns that match the node, and choosing the best amongst them. The chosen rule's template is then instantiated for the node. During the instantiation of a template, the node for which the template is being instantiated is called the current node. A template typically contains instructions that select an additional sequence of source nodes for processing. A sequence of source nodes is processed by appending the result tree structure created by processing each of the members of the sequence in order. The process of matching, instantiation and selection is continued recursively until no new source nodes are selected for processing.

Implementations are free to process the source document in any way that produces the same result as if it were processed using this processing model.

2.4 Data Model

XSL operates on an XML document, whether a stylesheet or a source document, as a tree. Any two stylesheets or source documents that have the same tree will be processed the same by XSL. The XML document resulting from the tree construction process is also a tree. This section describes how XSL models an XML document as a tree. This model is conceptual only and does not mandate any particular implementation.

XML documents operated on by XSL must conform to the XML namespaces specification [W3C XML Names].

The tree contains nodes. There are seven kinds of node:

- root nodes
- element nodes

- text nodes
- attribute nodes
- namespace nodes
- processing instruction nodes
- comment nodes

Neither processing instruction nodes nor comment nodes are included in the tree for the stylesheet.

For every type of node there is a way of determining a string value for a node of that type. For some types of node, the value is part of the node; for other types of node, the value is computed from the value of descendant nodes.

Issue (data-entity): Should XSL provide support for external data entities and notations?

2.4.1 Root Node

The root node is the root of the tree. It does not occur anywhere else in the tree. It has a single child which is the element node for the document element of the document.

The value of the root node is the value of the document element.

2.4.2 Element Nodes

There is an element node for every element in the document. An element has an expanded name consisting of a local name and a possibly null URI (see [W3C XML Names]); the URI will be null if the element type name has no prefix and there is no default namespace in scope.

The children of an element node are the element nodes and characters for its content. Entity references to both internal and external entities are expanded. Character references are resolved.

The descendants of an element node are the character children, the element node children, and the descendants of the element node children.

The value of an element node is the string that results from concatenating all characters that are descendants of the element node in the order in which they occur in the document.

The set of all element nodes in a document can be ordered according to the order of the start-tags of the elements in the document; this is known as document order.

2.4.2.1 Unique IDs

An element object may have a unique identifier (ID). This is the value of the attribute which is declared in the DTD as type ID. Since XSL must also work with XML documents that do not have a DTD, stylesheets may specify which attributes in the source document should be treated as IDs. The `xsl:id` element has a required attribute attribute, which gives the name of an attribute in the source document that should be treated as specifying the element's ID. A stylesheet may contain more than one `xsl:id` element, for cases where the source document uses several attributes as IDs. An `xsl:id` element also has an optional element attribute which specifies the name of an element type; when the element attribute is specified, then the `xsl:id` element specifies that the attribute attribute of element elements are treated as IDs. `xsl:id` elements may only occur in the stylesheet body (not within a rule). The following causes XSL to treat all name attributes in the source document as IDs.

```
<xsl:id attribute="name"/>
```

It is an error if, as a consequence of the use of `xsl:id`, there is more than one element with the same ID in the source tree. An XSL processor may signal the error; if it does not signal the error, it must recover by treating only the first (in document order) of the elements as having that ID.

> **Issue (-id-content)**: Should it be possible for a unique id to be specified in the content of an element instead of in an attribute?

2.4.2.2 Base URI

An element node also has an associated URI called its base URI which is used for resolving attribute values that represent relative URIs into absolute URIs. If an element occurs in an external entity, the base URI of that element is the URI of the external entity. Otherwise the base URI is the base URI of the document.

2.4.3 Attribute Nodes

Each element node has an associated set of attribute nodes. A defaulted attribute is treated the same as a specified attribute. If an attribute was declared for the element type, but the default was declared as `#IMPLIED`, and the attribute was not specified on the element, then the element's attribute set does not contain a node for the attribute.

An attribute node has an expanded name and has a string value. The expanded name consists of a local name and a possibly null URI (see [W3C XML Names]); the URI will be null if the specified attribute name did not have a prefix. The value is the normalized value as specified by the XML

Recommendation [W3C XML]. An attribute value whose value is of zero length is not treated specially.

There are no attribute nodes for attributes that declare namespaces (see [W3C XML Names]).

> **Issue (external-dtd):** Should we specify something about how we expect XSL processors to process external DTDs and parameter entities? For example, what happens if an attribute default is declared in an external DTD?

2.4.4 Namespace Nodes

Each element has an associated set of namespace nodes, one for each namespace prefix that is in scope for element and one for the default namespace if one is in scope for the element. This means that an element will have a namespace node:

- for every attribute on the element whose name starts with xmlns:;
- for every attribute on an ancestor element whose name starts xmlns: unless the element itself or a nearer ancestor redeclares the prefix;
- for an xmlns attribute, unless its value is the empty string.

> **NOTE:** An attribute xmlns=" " "undeclares" the default namespace (see [W3C XML Names]).

A namespace node has a name which is a string giving the prefix. This is empty if the namespace node is for the default namespace. A namespace node also has a value which is the namespace URI. If the namespace declaration specifies a relative URI, then the resolved absolute URI is used as the value.

When writing an element node in the result tree out as XML, an XSL processor must add sufficient namespace-declaring attributes to the start-tag to ensure that if a tree were recreated from the XML, then the set of namespace nodes on the element node in the recreated tree would be equal to or a superset of the set of namespace nodes of the element node in the result tree.

> **NOTE:** The semantics of a document type may treat parts of attribute values or data content as namespace prefixes. The presence of namespace nodes ensures that the semantics can be preserved when the tree is written out as XML.

2.4.5 Processing Instruction Nodes

There is a processing instruction node for every processing instruction.

> **Ed. Note**: What about processing instructions in the internal subset or elsewhere in the DTD?

A processing instruction has a name. This is a string equal to the processing instruction's target. It also has a value. This is a string equal to the part of the processing instruction following the target and any whitespace. It does not include the terminating ?>.

2.4.6 Comment Nodes

There is a comment node for every comment.

> **Ed. Note:** What about comments in the internal subset or elsewhere in the DTD?

A comment has a value. This is a string equal to the text of the comment not including the opening <!—or the closing—>.

2.4.7 Text Nodes

Character data is grouped into text nodes. As much character data as possible is grouped into each text node: a text node never has an immediately following or preceding sibling that is a text node. The value of a text node is the character data.

Each character within a CDATA section is treated as character data. Thus <![CDATA[<]]> in the source document will treated the same as <. Characters inside comments or processing instructions are not character data. Line-endings in external entities are normalized to #xA as specified in the XML Recommendation [W3C XML].

2.4.8 Whitespace Stripping

After the tree has been constructed, but before it is otherwise processed by XSL, some text nodes may be stripped. The stripping process takes as input a set of element types for which whitespace must be preserved. The stripping process is applied to both stylesheets and source documents, but the set of whitespace-preserving element types is determined differently for stylesheets and for source documents.

A text node is preserved if any of the following apply:

- The element type of the parent of the text node is in the set of whitespace-preserving element types.

- The text node contains at least one non-whitespace character. As in XML, a whitespace character is #x20, #x9, #xD or #xA.

- An ancestor element of the text node has an xml:space attribute with a value of preserve, and no closer ancestor element has xml:space with a value of default.

Otherwise the text node is stripped.

The xml:space attributes are not stripped from the tree.

> **NOTE**: This implies that if an xml:space attribute is specified on a literal result element, it will be included in the result.

For stylesheets, the set of whitespace-preserving element types consists of just xsl:text.

For source documents, the set of whitespace-preserving element types is determined using the stylesheet as follows:

- If the xsl:stylesheet element specifies a default-space attribute with a value of strip, then the set is initially empty. Otherwise the set initially contains all element types that occur in the document.

- The xsl:strip-space element causes an element type to be removed from the set of whitespace-preserving element types. The element attribute gives the name of the element type.

- The xsl:preserve-space element causes an element type to be added to the set whitespace-preserving element types. The element attribute gives the name of the element type.

Issue (declare-multiple-elements): Should the value of the element attribute of xsl:strip-space, xsl:preserve-space and xsl:id be a list of element type names (and thus be renamed to elements)? If so, should the attribute attribute of xsl:id also be a list of attribute names?

Ed. Note: Clarify how these declarations interact with each other and with xsl:import.

The xsl:stylesheet element can include an indent-result attribute with values yes or no. If the stylesheet specifies indent-result="yes", then the XSL processor may add whitespace to the result tree (possibly based on whitespace stripped from either the source document or the stylesheet) in order to indent the result nicely; if indent-result="no", it must not add any whitespace to the result. When adding whitespace with indent-result="yes", the XSL processor can use any algorithm provided that the result is the same as the result with indent-result="no" after whitespace is stripped from both using the process described with the set of whitespace-preserving element types consisting of just xsl:text.

2.5 Template Rules

A template rule is specified with the xsl:template element. The match attribute identifies the source node or nodes to which the rule applies. The content of the xsl:template element is the template.

For example, an XML document might contain:

This is an <emph>important</emph> point.

The following template rule matches elements of type emph and has a template which produces a fo:inline-sequence formatting object with a font-weight property of bold.

```
<xsl:template match="emph">

  <fo:inline-sequence font-weight="bold">
    <xsl:apply-templates/>
  </fo:inline-sequence>
</xsl:template>
```

As described later, the xsl:apply-templates element recursively processes the children of the source element.

2.5.1 Conflict Resolution for Template Rules

It is possible for a source node to match more than one template rule. The template rule to be used is determined as follows:

1. First, all matching template rules that are less important than the most important matching template rule or rules are eliminated from consideration.

2. Next, all matching template rules that have a lower priority than the matching template rule or rules with the highest priority are eliminated from consideration. The priority of a rule is specified by the priority attribute on the rule. The value of this must be a real number (positive or negative). The default priority is 0.

   Ed. Note: Say exactly what syntax is allowed for real numbers.

   Issue (default-priority): Should there be a more complicated way of calculating the default priority? For example, -1 for *, 0 for just an element type name, and 1 for more complex patterns.

It is an error if this leaves more than one matching template rule. An XSL processor may signal the error; if it does not signal the error, it must recover by choosing from amongst the matching template rules that are left the one that occurs last in the stylesheet.

2.5.2 Built-in Template Rules

There is a built-in template rule to allow recursive processing to continue in the absence of a successful pattern match by an explicit rule in the stylesheet. This rule applies to both element nodes and the root node. The following shows the equivalent of the built-in template rule:

```
<xsl:template match="*|/">
  <xsl:apply-templates/>
</xsl:template>
```

There is also a built-in template rule for text nodes that copies text through:

```
<xsl:template match="text()">
  <xsl:value-of select="."/>
</xsl:template>
```

The built-in rule does not apply to processing instructions and comments. When a comment or processing instruction is processed, and no rule is matched, nothing is created.

The built-in template rules are treated as if they were imported implicitly before the stylesheet and so are considered less important than all other template rules. Thus the author can override a built-in rule by including an explicit rule with match="*|/" or match="text()".

2.6 Patterns

2.6.1 Introduction

This section introduces the syntax and semantics of XSL patterns. The formal, definitive specification is in the following section.

A pattern is a string which selects a set of nodes in a source document. The selection is relative to the current node. The simplest pattern is an element type name; it selects all the child elements of the current node with that element type name. For example, the pattern chapter selects all the chapter child elements of the current node.

A pattern can also be matched against a node. If a node could be selected by a pattern, then the node is considered to match the pattern. More precisely, for any pattern and any document there is a matching set of nodes; this is the union, for each node in the document, of the set of nodes selected by the pattern with that node as the current node. For example, a pattern chapter matches any chapter element because if the current node was the parent of the chapter element, the chapter element would be one of the nodes selected by the pattern chapter. This includes the case where the chapter element is the document element, because the root node is the parent of the document element.

The | operator can be used to express alternatives. For example, the pattern emph|b matches both emph elements and b elements.

Patterns can be composed together with the / operator in a path-like manner. For example, a pattern chapter/section selects the chapter child elements of the current node, and then for each selected chapter element, selects the section children; in other words, it selects the section grandchildren of the current node that have chapter parents. A node would match a pattern `chapter/section` if it was a section element with a `chapter` parent.

/ binds more tightly than |. Thus the pattern ol/li|ul/li matches li elements that have an ol or ul parent.

Whitespace can be used around operators in patterns to improve readability. Thus ol/li|ul/li can be written as ol/li | ul/li.

* can be used instead of an element type name as a wildcard. For example, a pattern * would select all element children of the current node; a pattern */section would select all section grandchildren of the current node. A pattern chapter/* would match any element that has a chapter parent.

A // can be used instead of / to select from descendants instead of from children. For example, a pattern chapter//p selects all the p descendants of chapter children of the current node, and it matches all p elements that have a chapter ancestor.

A pattern . selects the current node. This is useful with //. For example, .//div selects all div descendant elements of the current node.

Similarily .. selects the parent of the current node. For example, ../item selects the item sibling elements of the current node.

Other types of node are treated in a similar way to elements.

- The attributes of an element are treated like the child elements; an attribute is distinguished from a child element by prefixing its name with @. For example, @date will select the date attribute of the current element; employee/@salary will select the salary attribute of each employee child element of the current node. A wildcard @* is allowed just as with elements; a pattern @* selects all attributes of the current node.

- A pattern comment ( ) selects all comment children of the current node. Thus a pattern comment ( ) will match any comment node.

- A pattern pi ( ) selects all processing instruction children of the current node. An argument can be used to specify the target. Thus pi ("xml-stylesheet") matches any processing instruction with a target xml-stylesheet. Note that the argument must be quoted.

The set of nodes selected by a pattern can be refined by following the pattern by a test in square brackets ([]). Each node in the set is tested. The result includes only those nodes for which a test succeeds. The following are allowed as tests:

- A pattern can be used a test; the test succeeds if the pattern selects one or more nodes when the node being tested is the current node. For example, a pattern list [@type] matches a list element with a type attribute; a pattern book [editor] selects book children elements of the current node that have at least one editor child element.

- A pattern can be compared to a string. For example, a pattern list [@type="ordered"] would match any list with an attribute type with value ordered; a pattern employee [location="USA"] would select employee children of the current element that have a location child with value equal to USA.

- The position of a node relative to its siblings can be tested.

  - first-of-any ( ) succeeds if the node being tested is the first element child

  - last-of-any ( ) succeeds if the node being tested is the last element child

  - first-of-type ( ) succeeds if the node being tested is the first element child of its element type

  - last-of-type ( ) succeeds if the node being tested is the first element child of its element type

- A test can be negated using not(). For example, list[not(@type)] matches any list element without a type attribute.

- Tests can be combined with and and or. For example,

  back/div`[first-of-type()` and `last-of-type()]`

  matches a `div` element with a `back` parent, when it is the only `div` child of its parent.

The `[]` operator binds more tightly than `|` . Thus the pattern ol|list[@type="ordered"] matches either list elements with a type attribute with value ordered or ol elements.

The root node is treated is specially. A / at the beginning of a pattern selects the root node (not the document element). For example, a pattern that is just / matches the root node; a pattern /div will match the document element it is a div element; a pattern /* will match the document element whatever is. When a pattern starts with / the current node is irrelevant.

A pattern can also start with `//` . `//foo` means the same as `/.//foo`: it selects the foo descendants of the root node, which implies that it selects all foo elements. When a pattern starts with `//` the current node is irrelevant.

The ancestor function allows selection of an `ancestor` of the current node. The argument is a match pattern. It selects the first `ancestor` of the current node that matches the argument. For example, ancestor`(chapter)/title` will select the title children of the first ancestor of the current node that is a `chapter`.

The id function allows ID references to be followed. The argument can be a literal string. For example, id('foo') will select the element with ID `foo`; if there is no such element, the empty node set will be returned. Multiple whitespace separated IDs are also allowed; this id('foo bar') would select elements with an ID `foo` or `bar`. The argument can be a pattern instead of a literal string; for each node selected by the pattern, the value of the node is treated as whitespace separated list of ID references. For example, if the current node is an element with an IDREF or IDREFS attribute named ref, then a pattern id(@ref) would select the elements referenced by the `ref` attribute.

   Ed. Note: Would it be less confusing to call this idref?

2.6.2 Syntax and Semantics

An expression is evaluated with respect to a context, which is a single node. The result of evaluating an expression is a set of nodes or a boolean.

In the following grammar, the nonterminal QName is defined in [W3C XML Names], and S is defined in [W3C XML].

Selecting

[1]	SelectExpr	::=	UnionExpr

select pattern must match the production for SelectExpr; it returns the list of nodes that results from evaluating the SelectExpr with the current node as context; the nodes are in the list are in document order.

Matching

[2]	MatchExpr	::=	SelectExpr

A *match pattern* must match the production for MatchExpr; a node matches the match pattern if the MatchExpr returns true when evaluated with that node as context.

The result of the MatchExpr is true if, for any node in the document that contains the context of the MatchExpr, the result of evaluating the SelectExpr with that node as context contains the context of the MatchExpr. Otherwise the result is false.

> **NOTE:** A practical implementation needs to provide direct support for evaluating a pattern as a MatchExpr, rather than supporting it indirectly in terms of the equivalent SelectExpr semantics. For example, to test whether a node matches a pattern foo, an implementation should not evaluate the pattern foo as a select pattern with each node in the source document as context, rather it should simply check whether the node is an element of type foo; to test whether a node matches a pattern foo//bar is should check whether the node is an element of type bar with an ancestor element of type foo.

Unions

[3]	UnionExpr	::=	PathExpr
			| (PathExpr '|' UnionExpr)

The context of the right hand side expressions is the context of the left hand side expression. The results of the right hand side expressions are node sets. The result of the left hand side UnionExpr is the union of the results of the right hand side expressions.

Paths

[4]	PathExpr	::=	AbsolutePathExpr
			| ComposeExpr

The context of the right hand side expressions is the context of the left hand side expression. The result of the left hand side is the result of the right hand side. The result is a node set.

Absolute Paths

[5]	AbsolutePathExpr	::=	'/' SubtreeExpr?

If the SubtreeExpr is present, then the context for the SubtreeExpr is the root node, and the result is the result of the SubtreeExpr. Otherwise the result is the root node.

Subtrees

[6]	SubtreeExpr	::=	'/'? ComposeExpr

If the / is present, then the result SubtreeExpr is the union, for each node in the subtree rooted at the context of the SubtreeExpr, of the result of evaluating the ComposeExpr with that node as context. Otherwise the SubtreeExpr is equivalent to ComposeExpr.

Composition

[7]	ComposeExpr	::=	FilterExpr
			| (FilterExpr '/' SubtreeExpr)

The context of the FilterExpr is the context of the ComposeExpr. If the SubtreeExpr is present, then, for each node in the result of the FilterExpr, the SubtreeExpr is evaluated with that node as the context; the result of the ComposeExpr is the union of the results of evaluating the SubtreeExpr. Otherwise the result is the result of the FilterExpr.

Filtering

[8]	FilterExpr	::=	NodeExpr ('[' BooleanExpr ']')?

The context of the NodeExpr is the context of the FilterExpr. If the BooleanExpr is present, then for each node in the result of the NodeExpr, the BooleanExpr is evaluated with that node as context; the result consists of those nodes for which the BooleanExpr evaluates to true.

Selecting Nodes

[9]	NodeExpr	::=	SubNodeExpr
			| OtherNodeExpr

[10]	SubNodeExpr	::=	ElementExpr
			| AttributeExpr
			| TextExpr
			| CommentExpr
			| PiExpr

[11]	OtherNodeExpr	::=	IdExpr
			| AncestorExpr
			| AncestorOrSelfExpr
			| IdentityExpr
			| ParentExpr

The context of the right hand side expressions is the context of the left hand side expression. The results of the right hand side expressions are node sets. The result of the left hand side is the result of the left hand side expression.

> **Issue (multiple-sources):** Should it be possible for patterns to select nodes in documents other than the source document?

Issue (sibling-qual): Should there be qualifiers that constrain an element to have an immediately preceding or following sibling of a particular type?

Elements

[12]	ElementExpr	::=	QName
			| '*'

If * is specified, then the result is the child elements of the context of the ElementExpr. Otherwise, the result is the set of all elements that are the children of the context of ElementExpr and whose name is equal to QName.

When comparing the name of an element to a QName, the QName is expanded into a local name and a possibly null URI. This expansion is done in the same way as for element type names in start and end-tags except that the default namespace declared with xmlns is not used: if the QName does not have a prefix, then the URI is null (this is the same way attribute names are expanded). The expanded element type names are compared (see Section 2.4.2: Element Nodes).

Issue (pattern-namespace-wildcards): Should patterns of the form foo:* or *:foo be allowed? If so, should * match any element or any element without a namespace URI?

Attributes

[13]	AttributeExpr	::=	('@' QName)
			| ('@' '*')

If * is specified, the result is the set of attribute nodes of the context of the AttributeExpr. If a QName is specified, the result is the attribute node of the context of the AttributeExpr named QName, or the empty node set if there is no such attribute node. When matching attribute names, the expanded names are compared (see Section 2.4.3: Attribute Nodes). The QName is expanded in the same way as a QName in an ElementExpr.

Issue (attribute-qual-case): Do we need to be able to match attributes in a case insensitive way?

Processing Instructions

[14]	PiExpr	::=	'pi' '(' Literal? ')'

If the Literal is present, the result is the set of processing instruction nodes which are children of the context of the PiExpr and whose target is equal to the value of Literal. Otherwise the result is the set of processing instruction nodes which are children of the context of the PiExpr.

Text

[15]	TextExpr	::=	'text' '(' ')'

The result is the set of all text nodes whose parent is a node in the context of the TextExpr.

> **Issue (regex):** Should XSL support regular expressions for matching against any or all of pcdata content, attribute values, attribute names, element type names?

Comments

[16]	CommentExpr	::=	'comment' '(' ')'

The result is the set of all comment nodes which are children of the context of the CommentExpr.

IDs

[17]	IdExpr	::=	ConstantIdExpr
			| VariableIdExpr

[18]	ConstantIdExpr	::=	'id' '(' Literal ')'

[19]	VariableIdExpr	::=	'id' '(' SelectExpr ')'

The context of the SelectExpr is the context of the IdExpr. A set of names is computed from the argument as follows:

- If it is a ConstantIdExpr, then the value of the Literal is treated as a whitespace-separated list of names; the set of names consists of the members of the list.

- Otherwise, the value of each node in the result of the SelectExpr is treated as a whitespace-separated list of names; the set of names is the union for each node of the members of the list.

The result is the set of element nodes whose ID (see Section 2.4.2.1: Unique IDs) is one of the names in the set of names specified by the argument.

Issue (class-attribute): Should there be a way of specifying that an attribute serves as a class attribute and then pattern syntax that treats class attributes specially?

Ancestors

[20]	AncestorExpr	::=	'ancestor' '(' MatchExpr ')'

[21]	AncestorOrSelfExpr	::=	'ancestor-or-self' '(' MatchExpr ')'

The result of an AncestorExpr is the first ancestor of the context of the AncestorExpr such that MatchExpr, when evaluated with that ancestor as the context, has a result of true. If there is no such ancestor, the result is the empty node set.

With ancestor-or-self, a node is treated as the first of its ancestors. Thus if the MatchExpr evaluates to true with the context of the AncestorOrSelfExpr, then the result of the AncestorOrSelfExpr is the context, otherwise the result is the same as the result of an AncestorExpr.

Identity

[22]	IdentityExpr	::=	'.'

The result is the context of the IdentityExpr.

Parents

[23]	ParentExpr	::=	'..'

The result is the parent of the context of the ParentExpr. If the context is the root node, then the result is the empty node set.

Boolean Expressions

[24]	BooleanExpr	::=	AndExpr
			| OrExpr
			| BooleanPrimaryExpr

[25]	BooleanPrimaryExpr	::=	BooleanGroupExpr
			| NotExpr
			| PositionalExpr
			| TestExpr

The result of a BooleanExpr is true or false. The context of the right hand side expressions is the context of the BooleanExpr. The result of the BooleanExpr is the result of the right hand side.

And

[26]	AndExpr	::=	BooleanPrimaryExpr ('and' BooleanPrimaryExpr)+

The context for each BooleanPrimaryExpr is the context of the AndExpr. The result is true if the result of all of the BooleanPrimaryExprs is true; otherwise the result is false.

Or

[27]	OrExpr	::=	BooleanPrimaryExpr ('or' BooleanPrimaryExpr)+

The context for each BooleanPrimaryExpr is the context of the OrExpr. The result is true if the result of any of the BooleanPrimaryExprs is true; otherwise the result is false.

Grouping

[28]	BooleanGroupExpr	::=	'(' BooleanExpr ')'

The result of the left hand side is the result of the right hand side. The context of the right hand side is the context of the left hand side.

Negation

[29]	NotExpr	::=	'not' '(' BooleanExpr ')'

The result of the NotExpr is true if the result of the BooleanExpr is false; otherwise the result is false.

Position

[30]	PositionalExpr	::=	'first-of-type' '(' ')'
			| 'last-of-type' '(' ')'
			| 'first-of-any' '(' ')'
			| 'last-of-any' '(' ')'

The context of the PositionalExpr is a single node.

- For first-of-type ( ), the result is true if the context node is an element and the element has no preceding siblings that are elements with the same element type name, and false otherwise.
- For first-of-any ( ), the result is true if the context node is an element and the element has no preceding siblings that are elements, and false otherwise.
- For last-of-type ( ), the result is true if the context node is an element and the element has no following siblings that are elements with the same element type name, and false otherwise.
- For last-of-any ( ), the result is true if the context node is an element and the element has no following siblings that are elements, and false otherwise.

Testing Existence

[31]	TestExpr	::=	SelectExpr

The context of the SelectExpr is the context of the EqualityExpr. The result of the TestExpr is true if the result of the SelectExpr is non-empty. Otherwise the result is false.

Equality

[32]	EqualityExpr	::=	SelectExpr '=' Literal

The context of the SelectExpr is the context of the EqualityExpr. The result is true if there is a node in the result of the SelectExpr whose value is equal to the value of the Literal.

Ed. Note: We plan to use the data-typing facilities being developed by the XML Schema WG to allow ordered comparisons.

Literal

[33]	Literal	::=	`"" [^"]* ""`
			`| "" [^']* ""`

The value of the Literal is the sequence of characters inside the " or " characters>.

Pattern Lexical Structure

[34]	PatternToken	::=	`'/' | '@' | '(' | ')' | '[' | '[' | ']' | '=' | '.' | '..' | '*`
			| QName
			| OperatorName
			| FunctionName
			| Literal

[35]	OperatorName	::=	'and'
			| 'or'

[36]	FunctionName	::=	'id'
			| 'ancestor'
			| 'ancestor-or-self'
			| 'comment'
			| 'pi'
			| 'text'
			| 'not'
			| 'first-of-type'
			| 'last-of-type'
			| 'first-of-any'
			| 'last-of-any'

[37]	PatternWhitespace	::=	S

For readability, whitespace may be used in patterns even though not explicitly allowed by the grammar: PatternWhitespace may be freely added within patterns before or after any PatternToken.

A FunctionName token is recognized only when the following token is (An OperatorName token is recognized only when there is a preceding token and the preceding token is not one of @, /, |, (, [or an OperatorName. A string that is equal to an OperatorName or a FunctionName can be used in an ElementExpr or an AttributeExpr. For example, and[not and or] matches a element named and with an element child named not and an element child named or.

2.7 Templates

2.7.1 Overview

When the rule that is to be applied to the source element has been identified, the rule's template is instantiated. A template can contain literal result elements, character data and instructions for creating fragments of the result tree. Instructions are represented by elements in the XSL namespace.

The xsl:apply-templates instruction can select descendant nodes for processing. Without any attribute, the xsl:apply-templates instruction processes the immediate children nodes of the source element; a select attribute can be used to process nodes selected by a specified pattern.

```
<xsl:template match="chapter/title">
  <fo:rule-graphic/>
  <fo:block space-before="2pt">
```

```
        <xsl:text>Chapter </xsl:text>
        <xsl:number/>
        <xsl:text>: </xsl:text>
        <xsl:apply-templates/>
      </fo:block>
      <fo:rule-graphic/>
    </xsl:template>
```

Issue (instruction-error): Should there be an instruction that generates an error, like the error procedure in DSSSL?

Issue (multiple-results): Should it be possible to create multiple result trees?

2.7.2 Creating Elements and Attributes

2.7.2.1 Literal Result Elements

In a template an element in the stylesheet that does not belong to the XSL namespace is instantiated to create an element node of the same type. The created element node will have the attribute nodes that were present on the element node in the stylesheet tree. The created element node will also have the namespace nodes that were present on the element node in the stylesheet tree with the exception of any namespace node whose value is the XSL namespace URI (http://www.w3.org/TR/WD-xsl).

The value of an attribute of a literal result element is interpreted as an attribute value template: it can contain string expressions contained in curly braces ({}).

Namespace URIs that occur literally in the stylesheet and that are being used to create nodes in the result tree can be quoted. This applies to:

- the namespace URI in the expanded name of an literal result element in the stylesheet
- the namespace URI in the expanded name of an attribute specified on a literal result element in the stylesheet
- the value of a namespace node on a literal result element in the stylesheet

A namespace URI is quoted by prefixing it with the string quote:. This prefix will be removed when the template is instantiated to create the result element node with its associated attribute nodes and namespace nodes.

When literal result elements are being used to create element, attribute, or namespace nodes that use the XSL namespace URI, the namespace must be quoted to avoid misinterpretation by the XSL processor.

NOTE: It may be necessary also to quote other namespaces. For example, literal result elements belonging to a namespace dealing with digital signatures might cause XSL stylesheets to be mishandled by general purpose security software; quoting the namespace would avoid the possibility of such mishandling.

For example, the stylesheet

```
<xsl:stylesheet
   xmlns:xsl="http://www.w3.org/TR/WD-xsl"
xmlns:fo="http://www.w3.org/TR/WD-xsl/FO"

   xmlns:qxsl="quote:http://www.w3.org/TR/WD-xsl">

<xsl:template match="/">
  <qxsl:stylesheet>
    <xsl:apply-templates/>
  </qxsl:stylesheet>
</xsl:template>

<xsl:template match="block">
  <qxsl:template match="{.}">
     <fo:block><qxsl:apply-templates/></fo:block>
  </qxsl:template>
</xsl:template>

</xsl:stylesheet>
```

will generate an XSL stylesheet from a document of the form:

```
<elements>
<block>p</block>
<block>h1</block>
<block>h2</block>
<block>h3</block>
<block>h4</block>
</elements>
```

2.7.2.2 Creating Elements with `xsl:element`

The xsl:element allows an element to be created with a computed name. The xsl:element element has a required name attribute that specifies the name of the element. The name attribute is interpreted as an attribute value template. It is instantiated to create an element with the specified name. The content of the xsl:element element is a template for the attributes and children of the created element.

The value of the name attribute after instantiation must have one of two forms:

- It can be a QName. In this case the name is expanded in the same way as an element type name using the namespace declarations in scope for the xsl:element element in the stylesheet.
- It can be a namespace URI followed by a # character followed by an NCName. This can be used conjunction with a NameExpr to compute a qualified name.

2.7.2.3 Creating Attributes with `xsl:attribute`

The xsl:attribute element can be used to add attributes to result elements whether created by literal result elements in the stylesheet or by xsl:element elements. The xsl:attribute element has a required name attribute that specifies the name of the attribute. The name attribute is interpreted as an attribute value template It adds an attribute node to the containing result element node. The content of the xsl:attribute element is a template for the value of the created attribute.

The following are all errors:

- Adding an attribute to an element after children have been added to it; implementations may either signal the error or ignore the attribute.
- Including nodes other than text nodes in the value of an attribute; implementations may either signal the error or ignore the added nodes.
- Adding an attribute that has the same name as an attribute already added; implementations may either signal the error or ignore the duplicate attribute.
- Adding an attribute to a node that is not an element; implementations may either signal the error or ignore the attribute.

2.7.2.4 Named Attribute Sets

The `xsl:attribute-set` element defines a named set of attributes. The name attribute specifies the name of the attribute set. The xsl:use element adds a named set of attributes to an element. It has a required attribute-set attribute that specifies the name of the attribute set. xsl:use is allowed in the same places as xsl:attribute. The content of the `xsl:attribute-set` consists of xsl:attribute elements that specify attributes; it may also contain xsl:use elements. The value of attributes in an attribute set is determined when the attribute set is used rather than when the attribute set is defined.

The following example creates a named attribute set title-style and uses it in a template rule.

```
<xsl:attribute-set name="title-style">
  <xsl:attribute name="font-size">12pt</xsl:attribute>
  <xsl:attribute name="font-weight">bold</xsl:attribute>
</xsl:attribute-set>

<xsl:template match="chapter/heading">
  <fo:block quadding="start">
    <xsl:use attribute-set="title-style"/>
    <xsl:apply-templates/>
  </fo:block>
</xsl:template>
```

Any attribute in a named attribute set specified by xsl:use is not added to an element if the element already has an attribute of that name.

Multiple definitions of an attribute set with the same name are merged. An attribute from a definition that is more important takes precedence over an attribute from a definition that is less important. It is an error if there are two attribute sets with the same name that are equally important and that both contain the same attribute unless there is a more important definition of the attribute set that also contains the attribute. An XSL processor may signal the error; if it does not signal the error, it must recover by choosing from amongst the most important definitions that specify the attribute the one that was specified last in the stylesheet.

Issue (attribute-set): Merging is the only functionality offered by attribute sets that is not provided by macros. Is this a sufficient reason to keep attribute sets?

2.7.3 Creating Text

A template can also contain text nodes. Each text node in a template remaining after whitespace has been stripped as specified in Section 2.4.8: Whitespace Stripping will create a text node with the same value in the result tree. Adjacent text nodes in the result tree are automatically merged.

Note that text is processed at the tree level. Thus, markup of < in a template will be represented in the stylesheet tree by a text node that includes the character <. This will create a text node in the result tree that contains a < character, which will be represented by the markup < (or an equivalent character reference) when the result tree is externalized as an XML document.

Literal data characters may also be wrapped in an xsl:text element. This wrapping may change what whitespace characters are stripped (see Section 2.4.8: Whitespace Stripping) but does not affect how the characters are handled by the XSL processor thereafter.

2.7.4 Creating Processing Instructions

The `xsl:pi` element is instantiated to create a processing instruction node. The content of the `xsl:pi` element is a template for the value of the processing instruction node. The `xsl:pi` element has a required name attribute that specifies the name of the processing instruction node. The value of the name attribute is interpreted as an attribute value template.

For example, this

```
<xsl:pi name="xml-stylesheet">href="book.css" type="text/css"</xsl:pi>
```
would create the processing instruction

```
<?xml-stylesheet href="book.css" type="text/css"?>
```
It is an error if instantiating the content of xsl:pi creates anything other than characters. An XSL processor may signal the error; if it does not signal the error, it must recover by ignoring the offending nodes together with their content.

It is an error if the result of instantiating the content of the xsl:pi contains the string ?>. An XSL processor may signal the error; if it does not signal the error, it must recover by inserting a space after any occurrence of ? that is followed by an >.

2.7.5 Creating Comments

The `xsl:comment` element is instantiated to create a comment node in the result tree. The content of the `xsl:comment` element is a template for the value of the comment node.

For example, this:

```
<xsl:comment>This file is automatically generated. Do not edit!</xsl:com-
ment>
```
would create the comment

```
<!—This file is automatically generated. Do not edit!—>
```

It is an error if instantiating the content of `xsl:comment` creates anything other than characters. An XSL processor may signal the error; if it does not signal the error, it must recover by ignoring the offending nodes together with their content.

It is an error if if the result of instantiating the content of the `xsl:comment` contains the string—or ends with—An XSL processor may signal the error; if it does not signal the error, it must recover by inserting a space after any occurrence of–that is followed by another—.

2.7.6 Processing with Template Rules

This example creates a block for a chapter element and then processes its immediate children.

```
<xsl:template match="chapter">
  <fo:block>
    <xsl:apply-templates/>
  </fo:block>
</xsl:template>
```

In the absence of a select attribute, the xsl:apply-templates instruction processes all of the children of the current node, including text nodes. However, text nodes that have been stripped as specified in Section 2.4.8: Whitespace Stripping will not be processed.

Ed. Note: There is no WG consensus on the use xsl:apply-templates without a select attribute to process all children of a node.

A select attribute can be used to process nodes selected by a pattern instead of all children. The value of the select attribute is a select pattern. The following example processes all of the author children of the author-group:

```
<xsl:template match="author-group">
  <fo:inline-sequence>
    <xsl:apply-templates select="author"/>
  </fo:inline-sequence>
</xsl:template>
```

The pattern controls the depth at which matches occur. The following example processes all of the first-names of the authors that are direct children of author-group:

```
<xsl:template match="author-group">
  <fo:inline-sequence>
```

```
    <xsl:apply-templates select="author/first-name"/>
  </fo:inline-sequence>
</xsl:template>
```

// can be used in the pattern to allow the matches to occur at arbitrary depths.

This example processes all of the heading elements contained in the book element.

```
<xsl:template match="book">
  <fo:block>
    <xsl:apply-templates select=".//heading"/>
  </fo:block>
</xsl:template>
```

An AncestorExpr in the pattern allows the processing of elements that are not descendants of the current node. This example finds an employee's department and then processes the group children of the department.

```
<xsl:template match="employee">
  <fo:block>
    Employee <xsl:apply-templates select="name"/> belongs to group
    <xsl:apply-templates select="ancestor(department)/group"/>
  </fo:block>
</xsl:template>
```

This example assumes that a department element contains group and employee elements (at some level). When processing the employee elements, the AncestorExpr in the pattern allows navigation upward to the department element in order to extract the information about the group to which the employee belongs.

An IdExpr allows processing of elements with a specific ID. For example, this template rule applies to elements with the ID cfo; the second xsl:apply-templates element processes the name child of the element with ID ceo:

```
<xsl:template match="id(cfo)">
    <xsl:apply-templates  select="name"/>  reports  to  <xsl:apply-templates
select="id(ceo)/name"/>
</xsl:template>
```

Multiple xsl:apply-templates elements can be used within a single template to do simple reordering. The following example creates two HTML tables. The first table is filled with domestic sales while the second table is filled with foreign sales.

```
<xsl:template match="product">
  <TABLE>
    <xsl:apply-templates select="sales/domestic"/>
  </TABLE>
  <TABLE>
    <xsl:apply-templates select="sales/foreign"/>
  </TABLE>
</xsl:template>
```

NOTE: It is possible for there to be two matching descendants where one is a descendant of the other. This case is not treated specially: both descendants will be processed as usual. For example, given a source document

```
<doc><div><div></div></div></doc>
```
the rule

```
<xsl:template match="doc">
  <xsl:apply-templates select=".//div"/>
</xsl:template>
```

will process both the outer div and inner div elements.

Use of select patterns in xsl:apply-templates can lead to infinite loops. It is an error if, during the invocation of a rule for an element, that same rule is invoked again for that element. An XSL processor may signal the error; if it does not signal the error, it must recover by creating an empty result tree structure for the nested invocation.

Issue (select-function): What mechanisms should be provided for selecting elements for processing? For example, how can elements specified indirectly be handled? Suppose there's an xref element with a ref attribute that specifies the ID of a div element. The template for xref needs to select title child of the div element referenced by the ref attribute. Should it be possible to select elements in other XML documents?

2.7.7 Direct Processing

When the result has a known regular structure, it is useful to be able to specify directly the template for selected nodes. The xsl:for-each element contains a template which is instantiated for each node selected by the pattern specified by the select attribute. The template is instantiated with the selected node as the current node.

For example, given an XML document with this structure

```
<customers>
  <customer>
    <name>...</name>
    <order>...</order>
    <order>...</order>
  </customer>
  <customer>
    <name>...</name>
    <order>...</order>
    <order>...</order>
  </customer>
</customers>
```

the following would create an HTML document containing a table with a row for each customer element

```
<xsl:template match="/">
    <HTML>
      <HEAD>
        <TITLE>Customers</TITLE>
      </HEAD>
      <BODY>
        <TABLE>
    <TBODY>
        <xsl:for-each select="customers/customer">
          <TR>
            <TH>
        <xsl:apply-templates select="name"/>
          </TH>
          <xsl:for-each select="order">
        <TD>
```

```
              <xsl:apply-templates/>
          </TD>
            </xsl:for-each>
          </TR>
        </xsl:for-each>
      </TBODY>
        </TABLE>
      </BODY>
    </HTML>
  </xsl:template>
```

As with `xsl:apply-templates` the pattern is a select pattern. The select attribute is required.

2.7.8 Processing Modes

Processing modes allow an element to be processed multiple times, each time producing a different result.

Both `xsl:template` and `xsl:apply-templates` have an optional mode attribute whose value is a name. If an xsl:apply-templates element has a mode attribute, then it applies only those template rules from `xsl:template` elements that have a mode attribute with the same value; if an xsl:apply-templates element does not have a mode attribute, then it applies only those template rules from `xsl:template` elements that do not have a a mode attribute.

If there is no matching template, then the built-in template rules are applied, even if a mode attribute was specified in `xsl:apply-templates`.

Ed. Note: Add some examples.

2.7.9 Sorting

Sorting is specified by adding xsl:sort elements as children of `xsl:apply-templates` or `xsl:for-each`. The first `xsl:sort` child specifies the primary sort key, the second xsl:sort child specifies the secondary sort key and so on. When `xsl:apply-templates` or `xsl:for-each` has one or more xsl:sort children, then instead of processing the selected elements in document order, it sorts the elements according to the specified sort keys and then processes them in sorted order. When used in `xsl:for-each`, `xsl:sort` elements must occur first.

`xsl:sort` has a select attribute whose value is a select pattern. For each node to be processed, the select pattern is evaluated with that node as the current node. The value of the first selected node is used as the sort key for that node. The default value of the code select attribute is . (which addresses the current node).

This string serves as a sort key for the node. The following optional attributes on `xsl:sort` control how the list of sort keys are sorted:

- order specifies whether the strings should be sorted in ascending or descending order; ascending specifies ascending order; descending specifies descending order; the default is ascending

- lang specifies the language of the sort keys; it has the same range of values as `xml:lang`[W3C XML]; if no lang value is specified, the language should be determined from the system environment

- data-type specifies the data type of the strings; the following values are allowed

  - text specifies that the sort keys should be sorted lexicographically in the culturally correct manner for the language specified by lang

  - number specifies that the sort keys should be converted to numbers and then sorted according to the numeric value; the value specified by lang can be used to assist in the conversion to numbers

The default value is text.

> **Ed. Note**: We plan to leverage the work on XML schemas to define further values in the future.

- case-order has the value upper-first or lower-first; this applies when data-type=`"text"`, and specifies that upper-case characters should sort before lower-case letters or vice-versa respectively. For example, if lang=`"en"` then A a B b are sorted with case-order=`"upper-first"` and a A b B are sorted with case-order=`"lower-first"`. The default value is language dependent.

Ed. Note: We plan also to add an attribute whose value is a label identifying the sorting scheme, to be specified by the I18N WG.

The values of all of the above attributes are interpreted as attribute value templates.

NOTE: It is recommended that implementors consult [UNICODE TR10] for information on internationalized sorting.

The sort must be stable: in the sorted list of nodes, any sublist that has sort keys that all compare equal must be in document order.

For example, suppose an employee database has the form

```
<employees>
  <employee>
    <name>
      <first>James</first>
      <last>Clark</last>
    </name>
    ...
  </employee>
</employees>
```

Then a list of employees sorted by name could be generated using:

```
<xsl:template match="employees">
 <ul>
   <xsl:apply-templates select="employee">
     <xsl:sort select="name/last"/>
     <xsl:sort select="name/first"/>
   </xsl:apply-templates>

 </ul>
</xsl:template>

<xsl:template match="employee">
 <li>
   <xsl:value-of select="name/first"/>
   <xsl:text> </xsl:text>
   <xsl:value-of select="name/last"/>
 </li>
</xsl:template>
```

2.7.10 Numbering

2.7.10.1 Numbering in the Source Tree

The xsl:number element does numbering based on the position of the current node in the source tree.

The `xsl:number` element can have the following attributes:

- The level attribute specifies what levels of the source tree should be considered; it has the values single, multi or any. The default is single.
- The count attribute is a match pattern that specifies what elements should be counted at those levels. The count attribute defaults to the element type name of the current node.
- The from attribute is a match pattern that specifies where counting starts from.

In addition the `xsl:number` element has the attributes specified in Section 2.7.10.3: Number to String Conversion Attributes for number to string conversion.

The `xsl:number` element first constructs a list of positive integers using the level, count and from attributes:

- When level="single", it goes up to the nearest ancestor (including the current node as its own ancestor) that matches the count pattern, and constructs a list of length one containing one plus the number of preceding siblings of that ancestor that match the count pattern. If there is no such ancestor, it constructs an empty list. If the from attribute is specified, then the only ancestors that are searched are those that are descendants of the nearest ancestor that matches the from pattern.
- When level="multi", it constructs a list of all ancestors of the current node in document order followed by the element itself; it then selects from the list those elements that match the count pattern; it then maps each element of the list to one plus the number of preceding siblings of that element that match the count pattern. If the from attribute is specified, then the only ancestors that are searched are those that are descendants of the nearest ancestor that matches the from pattern.
- When level="any", it constructs a list of length one containing one plus the number of elements at any level of the document that start before this node and that match the count pattern. If the from attribute is specified, then only elements after the first element before this element that match the from pattern are considered.

The list of numbers is then converted into a string using the attributes specified in Section 2.7.10.3: Number to String Conversion Attributes; when used with xsl:number the value of each of these attributes is interpreted as an attribute value template. After conversion, the resulting string is inserted in the result tree.

Ed. Note: Allowing them to be attribute value templates isn't consistent with the current DTD: the declared values would all have to be CDATA, and we couldn't use `xml:lang` because the XML spec doesn't allow the value to be expressed as a template.

The following would number the items in an ordered list:

```
<xsl:template match="ol/item">
  <fo:block>
    <xsl:number/><xsl:text>. </xsl:text><xsl:apply-templates/>
  </fo:block>
<xsl:template>
```

The following two rules would number title elements. This is intended for a document that contains a sequence of chapters followed by a sequence of appendices, where both chapters and appendices contain sections which in turn contain subsections. Chapters are numbered 1, 2, 3; appendices are numbered A, B, C; sections in chapters are numbered 1.1, 1.2, 1.3; sections in appendices are numbered A.1, A.2, A.3.

```
<xsl:template match="title">
  <fo:block>
    <xsl:number level="multi"
                count="chapter|section|subsection"
                format="1.1. "/>
    <xsl:apply-templates/>
  </fo:block>
</xsl:template>

<xsl:template match="appendix//title" priority="1">
  <fo:block>
    <xsl:number level="multi"
                count="appendix|section|subsection"
                format="A.1. "/>
    <xsl:apply-templates/>
  </fo:block>
</xsl:template>
```

The following example numbers notes sequentially within a chapter:

```
<xsl:template match="note">
  <fo:block>
    <xsl:number level="any" from="chapter" format="(1) "/>
    <xsl:apply-templates/>
  </fo:block>
</xsl:template>
```

The following example would number H4 elements in HTML with a three-part label:

```
<xsl:template match="H4">
 <fo:block>
   <xsl:number level="any" from="H1" count="H2"/>
   <xsl:text>.</xsl:text>
   <xsl:number level="any" from="H2" count="H3"/>
   <xsl:text>.</xsl:text>
   <xsl:number level="any" from="H3" count="H4"/>
   <xsl:text> </xsl:text>
   <xsl:apply-templates/>
 </fo:block>
</xsl:template>
```

2.7.10.2 Numbering in the Result Tree

The root node of the result and each result element has a set of named counters (a mapping from names to integers).

Counter values are inserted using xsl:counter and xsl:counters elements. The name of the counter is specified with the name attribute. xsl:counter first constructs a list of length one containing the value of the named counter from the nearest ancestor in the result tree that has a counter with the specified name; xsl:counters first constructs a list containing, for each ancestor in the result tree that has a counter with the specified name, the value of named counter from that ancestor. xsl:counter and xsl:counters then convert the list of numbers into a string using the attributes specified in Section 2.7.10.3: Number to String Conversion Attributes; when used with xsl:counter and xsl:counters the value of each of these attributes is interpreted as an attribute value template.

> **Ed. Note:** The use of attribute value templates here the same problem noted for their use in the previous section.

Counters are incremented using the xsl:counter-increment element. The name attribute specifies the name of the counter to be incremented. It finds the nearest ancestor in the result tree that has a counter with the specified name and increments that; if there is no such ancestor, it adds a counter with that name and a value of zero to the document root and then increments it. The counter is incremented by 1 by default, but this can be changed using the amount attribute; the value can be any integer.

The xsl:counter-reset element sets the value of a counter in the current named counter set. The current named counter set is the set of named counters of the containing element in the result tree or of the document root if there is no containing element. If the current named counter set does-n't contain a counter of that name, a counter is added to it, otherwise the existing value is changed. The name of the counter to be set is specified by the name attribute. The value to set it to is speci-fied by the value attribute; the value can be any integer; it defaults to 0.

The xsl:counter-scope element is a phantom result element: it behaves just like a normal result element for the purposes of result numbering in that it is considered part of the result tree and has a set of named counters, but doesn't actually create a result element. This is for when the result tree doesn't have enough structure for counting.

NOTE: The numbering may be performed in the tree construction process or may be left for the formatting process.

NOTE: These facilities for result tree numbering are based on the facilities for automatic num-bering in [CSS2].

The following example would number notes sequentially throughout a document:

```
<xsl:template match="note">
  <xsl:text> (Note </xsl:text>
  <xsl:counter-increment name="note"/>
  <xsl:counter name="note"/>
  <xsl:text>).</xsl:text>
</xsl:template>
```

The following would turn ordered lists into definition lists:

```
<xsl:template match="OL">
  <dl>
<xsl:counter-reset name="li"/>

    <xsl:apply-templates/>
  </dl>
</xsl:template>

<xsl:template match="LI">
  <xsl:counter-increment name="li"/>
  <dt><xsl:counter name="li"/></dt>
  <dd><xsl:apply-templates/></dd>
</xsl:template>
```

The following would do HTML style numbering:

```
<xsl:template match="h2">
  <xsl:counter-increment name="h2"/>
  <p>
    <xsl:counter name="h2"/>
    <xsl:text>. </xsl:text>
    <xsl:apply-templates/>
  </p>
  <xsl:counter-reset name="h3"/>
</xsl:template>

<xsl:template match="h3">
  <xsl:counter-increment name="h3"/>
  <p>
    <xsl:counter name="h2"/>
    <xsl:text>.</xsl:text>
    <xsl:counter name="h3"/>
    <xsl:text>. </xsl:text>
    <xsl:apply-templates/>
  </p>
  <xsl:counter-reset name="h4"/>
</xsl:template>
<xsl:template match="h4">
  <xsl:counter-increment name="h4"/>
  <p>
    <xsl:counter name="h2"/>
    <xsl:text>.</xsl:text>
    <xsl:counter name="h3"/>
    <xsl:text>.</xsl:text>
    <xsl:counter name="h4"/>
    <xsl:text>.</xsl:text>
    <xsl:apply-templates/>
  </p>
</xsl:template>
```

The following would deal with recursive divs each with a title child:

```
<xsl:template match="div">
  <div>
    <xsl:apply-templates/>
  </div>
</xsl:template>

<xsl:template match="title">
 <p>
  <xsl:counter-increment name="div"/>
  <xsl:counters name="div" format="1.1. "/>
  <xsl:apply-templates/>
 </p>
<xsl:counter-reset name="div"/>

</xsl:template>
```

2.7.10.3 Number to String Conversion Attributes

The following attributes are used to control conversion of a list of numbers into a string. The numbers are integers greater than 0. The attributes are all optional.

The main attribute is format. The default value for the format attribute is 1. The format attribute is split into a sequence of tokens where each token is a maximal sequence of alphanumeric characters or a maximal sequence of non-alphanumeric characters. Alphanumeric means any character that has a Unicode category of Nd, Nl, No, Lu, Ll, Lt, Lm or Lo. The alphanumeric tokens (format tokens) specify the format to be used for each number in the list. If the first token is a non-alphanumeric token, then the constructed string will start with that token; if the last token is non-alphanumeric token, then the constructed string will end with that token. Non-alphanumeric tokens that occur between two format tokens are separator tokens that are used to join numbers in the list. The n-th format token will be used to format the n-th number in the list. If there are more numbers than format tokens, then the last format token will be used to format remaining numbers. If there are no format tokens, then a format token of 1 is used to format all numbers. The format token specifies the string to be used to represent the number 1. Each number after the first will be separated from the preceding number by the separator token preceding the format token used to format that number, or, if there are no separator tokens, then by ..

Format tokens are a superset of the allowed values for the type attribute for the OL element in HTML 4.0 and are interpreted as follows:

- Any token where the last character has a decimal digit value of 1 (as specified in the Unicode 2.0 character property database), and the Unicode value of preceding characters is one less than the Unicode value of the last character. This generates a decimal representation of the number where each number is at least as long as the format token. Thus a format token 1 generates the sequence 1 2...10 11 12..., and a format token 01 generates the sequence 01 02...09 10 11 12...99 100 101.

- A format token A generates the sequence A B C...Z AA AB AC...

- A format token a generates the sequence a b c...z aa ab ac...

- A format token i generates the sequence i ii iii iv v vi vii vii ix x ...

- A format token I generates the sequence I II III IV V VI VII VII IX X ...

- Any other format token indicates a numbering sequence that starts with that token. If an implementation does not support a numbering system that starts with that token, it must use a format token of 1.

When numbering with an alphabetic sequence, the xml:lang attribute specifies which language's alphabet is to be used.

> **NOTE:** This can be considered as specifying the language of the value of the format attribute and hence is consistent with the semantics of xml:lang.

The letter-value attribute disambiguates between numbering schemes that use letters. In many languages there are two commonly used numbering schemes that use letters. One numbering scheme assigns numeric values to letters in alphabetic sequence, and the other assigns numeric values to each letter in some other manner. In English, these would correspond to the numbering sequences specified by the format tokens a and i. In some languages the first member of each sequence is the same, and so the format token alone would be ambiguous. A value of alphabetic specifies the alphabetic sequence; a value of other specifies the other sequence.

The digit-group-sep attribute gives the separator between groups of digits, and the optional n-digits-per-group specifies the number of digits per group. For example, digit-group-sep=" , " and n-digits-per-group=" 3 " would produce numbers of the form 1,000,000.

The sequence-src attribute gives the URI of a text resource that contains a whitespace separated list of the members of the numbering sequence.

> **Ed. Note:** Specify what should happen when the sequence runs out.

Here are some examples of conversion specifications:

- `format="&#x30A2;"` specifies Katakana numbering
- `format="&#x30A4;"` specifies Katakana numbering in the "iroha" order
- `format="&#x0E51;"` specifies numbering with Thai digits
- `format="&#x05D0;"` letter-value="other" specifies "traditional" Hebrew numbering
- `format="&#x10D0;"` letter-value="other" specifies Georgian numbering
- `format="&#x03B1;"` letter-value="other" specifies "classical" Greek numbering
- `format="&#x0430;"` letter-value="other" specifies Old Slavic numbering

2.7.11 Conditionals within a Template

There are two instructions in XSL which support conditional processing in a template: `xsl:if` and `xsl:choose`. The `xsl:if` instruction provides simple if-then conditionality; the `xsl:choose` instruction supports selection of one choice when there are several possibilities.

2.7.11.1 Conditional Processing with xsl:if

The `xsl:if` element has a single attribute, test which specifies a select pattern. The content is a template. If the pattern selects a non-empty list of elements, then the content is instantiated; otherwise nothing is created. In the following example, the names in a group of names are formatted as a comma separated list:

```
<xsl:template match="namelist/name">
  <xsl:apply-templates/>
  <xsl:if test=".[not(last-of-type())]">, </xsl:if>
</xsl:template>
```

Issue (condition-test): What should be the name and allowed value of the attribute that specifies the condition on `xsl:if` and `xsl:when`? Should it be generalized to allow anything that is allowed within [] ? Should it be a match pattern rather than a select pattern?

2.7.11.2 Conditional Processing with xsl:choose

The `xsl:choose` element selects one among a number of possible alternatives. It consists of a series of `xsl:when` elements followed by an optional `xsl:otherwise` element. Each `xsl:when` element has a single attribute, test, which specifies a select pattern; the test is treated as true if the pattern selects a non-empty list of elements. The content of the xsl:when and xsl:otherwise elements is a template. When an xsl:choose element is processed, each of the xsl:when elements is tested in turn. The content of the first, and only the first, xsl:when element whose test is true is instantiated. If no xsl:when is true, the content of the xsl:otherwise element is instantiated. If no xsl:when element is true, and no xsl:otherwise element is present, nothing is created.

The following example enumerates items in an ordered list using arabic numerals, letters, or roman numerals depending on the depth to which the ordered lists are nested.

```
<xsl:template match="orderedlist/listitem">
  <fo:list-item indent-start='2pi'>
    <fo:list-item-label>
      <xsl:choose>
        <xsl:when test='ancestor(orderedlist/orderedlist)'>
          <xsl:number format="i"/>
        </xsl:when>
        <xsl:when test='ancestor(orderedlist)'>
          <xsl:number format="a"/>
        </xsl:when>
        <xsl:otherwise>
          <xsl:number format="1"/>
        </xsl:otherwise>
      </xsl:choose>
      <xsl:text>. </xsl:text>
    </fo:list-item-label>
    <fo:list-item-body>
      <xsl:apply-templates/>
    </fo:list-item-body>
  </fo:list-item>
</xsl:template>
```

Issue (if-when-unify): Should xsl:if and xsl:when be unified into a single element?

2.7.12 Copying

The xsl:copy element provides an easy way of copying the current node. The xsl:copy element is replaced by a copy of the current node. The namespace nodes of the current node are automatically copied as well, but the attributes and children of the node are not automatically copied. The content of the `xsl:copy` element is a template for the attributes and children of the created node; the content is not used for nodes of types that do not have attributes or children (attributes, text, comments and processing instructions).

The root node is treated specially because the root node of the result tree is created implicitly. When the current node is the root node, `xsl:copy` will not create a root node, but will just use the content template.

For example, the identity transformation can be written using `xsl:copy` as follows:

```
<xsl:template match="*|@*|comment()|pi()|text()">
  <xsl:copy>
    <xsl:apply-templates select="*|@*|comment()|pi()|text()"/>
  </xsl:copy>
</xsl:template>
```

2.7.13 Computing Generated Text

Within a template, the `xsl:value-of` element can be used to compute generated text, for example by extracting text from the source tree or by inserting the value of a string constant. The `xsl:value-of` element does this with a string expression that is specified as the value of the select attribute. String expressions can also be used inside attribute values of literal result elements by enclosing the string expression in curly brace ({}).

2.7.13.1 String Expressions

String Expressions

[38]	StringExpr	::=	SelectExpr
				NameExpr
				ConstantRef
				MacroArgRef

The value of a string expression that is a pattern is the value of the first node selected by the pattern. The value of each kind of node is described in Section 2.4: Data Model. If no nodes are selected by the pattern, then the value is the empty string. The pattern is a select pattern.

> **Issue (resolve-expr):** Do we need a resolve(pattern) string expression that treats the characters as a relative URI and turns it into an absolute URI using the base URI of the addressed node?

Name Expression

[39]	NameExpr	::=	'name' '(' SelectExpr ')'

The value of a NameExpr is the expanded name of the first node selected by the SelectExpr. If no nodes are selected or the first node does not have a name, then the value is the empty string. If the expanded name has a null URI, then the value is just the local name. If the expanded name has a non-null URI, the value is the URI followed by the character # followed by the local name.

2.7.13.2 Using String Expressions with xsl:value-of

The xsl:value-of element is replaced by the value of the string expression specified by the select attribute. The select attribute is required.

For example, the following creates an HTML paragraph from a person element with first-name and surname attributes.

```
<xsl:template match="person">
  <P>
   <xsl:value-of select="@first-name"/>
   <xsl:text> </xsl:text>
   <xsl:value-of select="@surname"/>
  </P>
</xsl:template>
```

For example, the following creates an HTML paragraph from a person element with first-name and surname children elements.

```
<xsl:template match="person">
  <P>
   <xsl:value-of select="first-name"/>
   <xsl:text> </xsl:text>
   <xsl:value-of select="surname"/>
  </P>
</xsl:template>
```

The following precedes each procedure element with a paragraph containing the security level of the procedure. It assumes that the security level that applies to a procedure is determined by a security attribute on an ancestor element of the procedure. It also assumes that if more than one ancestor has a security attribute then the security level is determined by the closest such ancestor of the procedure.

```
<xsl:template match="procedure">
  <fo:block>
    <xsl:value-of select="ancestor(*[@security])/@security"/>
  </fo:block>
  <xsl:apply-templates/>
</xsl:template>
```

Issue (inherited-attribute): Unless an element counts as one of its own ancestors, using ancestor(*[@security])/@security won't work to get the inherited value of an attribute. We could either say ancestor always includes the current node; alternatively we could provide a variant of ancestor that does include the current node; alternatively we could provide a select pattern of the form inherited-attribute(`security').

2.7.13.3 Attribute Value Templates

In an attribute value that is interpreted as an *attribute value template,* such as an attribute of a literal result element, string expressions can be used by surrounding the string expression with curly braces ({}). The attribute value template is instantiated by replacing the string expression together with surrounding curly braces by the value of the string expression.

The following example creates an IMG result element from a photograph element in the source; the value of the SRC attribute of the IMG element is computed from the value of the image-dir constant and the content of the href child of the photograph element; the value of the WIDTH attribute of the IMG element is computed from the value of the width attribute of the size child of the photograph element:

```
<xsl:constant name="image-dir" value="/images"/>
<xsl:template match="photograph">
<IMG SRC="{constant(image-dir)}/{href}" WIDTH="{size/@width}"/>
</xsl:template>
```

With this source

```
<photograph>
  <href>headquarters.jpg</href>
  <size width="300"/>
</photograph>
```

the result would be

```
<IMG SRC="/images/headquarters.jpg" WIDTH="300"/>
```

When an attribute value template is instantiated, a double left or right curly brace outside a string expression will be replaced by a single curly brace. It is an error if a right curly brace occurs in an attribute value template outside a string expression without being followed by a second right curly brace; an XSL processor may signal the error or recover by treating the right curly brace as if it had been doubled. A right curly brace inside an Literal in a string expression is not recognized as terminating the string expression.

Curly braces are *not* recognized recursively inside string expressions. For example:

```
<a href="#{id({@ref})/title}">
```

is *not* allowed. Instead use simply:

```
<a href="#{id(@ref)/title}">
```

2.7.14 String Constants

Global string constants may be defined using an xsl:constant element. The name attribute specifies the name of the constant, and the value attribute specified the value.

> **Issue (constant-value):** Should the value of the constant be specified in the content of the xsl:constant element rather than by a value attribute?

A stylesheet must not contain more than one definition of a constant with the same name and same importance. A definition of a constant will not be used if there is another definition of a constant with the same name and higher importance.

String constants are referenced using a ConstantRef string expression.

String Constant References

[40]	ConstantRef	::=	'constant' '(' NCName ')'

```
<xsl:constant name="para-font-size" value="12pt"/>
<xsl:template match="para">
 <fo:block font-size="{constant(para-font-size)}">
```

```
    <xsl:apply-templates/>
  </fo:block>
</xsl:template>
```

Issue (local-constants): Should there be a way to define local constants?

The value attribute is interpreted as an attribute value template. If the value of a constant definition x references a constant y, then the value for y must be computed before the value of x. It is an error if it is impossible to do this for all constant definitions because of dependency cycles.

2.7.15 Macros

Issue (macro-name): Should macros be called something else?

Parts of templates can also be factored out of similar rules into macros for reuse. Macros allow authors to create aggregate result fragments and refer to the composite as if it were a single object. In this example, a macro is defined for a boxed paragraph with the word "Warning!" preceding the contents. The macro is referenced from a rule for warning elements.

```
<xsl:macro name="warning-para">
  <fo:block-level-box>
    <fo:block>
      <xsl:text>Warning! </xsl:text>
      <xsl:contents/>
    </fo:block>
  </fo:block-level-box>
</xsl:macro>
<xsl:template match="warning">
  <xsl:invoke macro="warning-para">
    <xsl:apply-templates/>
  </xsl-invoke>
</xsl:template>
```

Macros are defined using the macro element. The name attribute specifies the name of the macro being defined. The content of the macro element is a template, called the body of the macro. A macro is invoked using the xsl:invoke element; the content of xsl:invoke is a template. The name of the macro to be invoked is given by the macro attribute. Invoking a macro first instantiates the content of xsl:invoke. It then instantiates the body of the invoked macro passing it the result tree fragment created by the instantiation of the content of xsl:invoke; this fragment can be inserted in the body of the macro using the xsl:contents element.

Macros allow named arguments to be declared with the xsl:macro-arg element; the name attribute specifies the argument name, and the optional default attribute specifies the default value for the argument. Within the body of a macro, macro arguments are referenced using a MacroArgRef string expression. It is an error to refer to a macro argument that has not been declared. An XSL processor may signal the error; if it does not signal the error, it must recover by using an empty string. Arguments are supplied to a macro invocation using the code xsl:arg element; the name attribute specifies the argument name, and the value attribute specifies the argument value. It is an error to supply an argument to a macro invocation if the macro did not declare an argument of that name. An XSL processor may signal the error; if it does not signal the error, it must recover by ignoring the argument. The value attribute of xsl:arg and the default attribute of xsl:macro-arg are interpreted as attribute value templates; they can contain string expressions in curly braces as with literal result elements.

Macro Argument References

[41]	MacroArgRef	::=	'arg' '(' NCName ')'

This example defines a macro for a numbered-block with an argument to control the format of the number.

```
<xsl:macro name="numbered-block">
  <xsl:macro-arg name="format" default="1. "/>
  <xsl:number format="{arg(format)}"/>
  <fo:block/>
    <xsl:contents/>
  </fo:block>
</xsl:macro>

<xsl:template match="appendix/title">
  <xsl:invoke macro="numbered-block">
    <xsl:arg name="format" value="A. "/>
    <xsl:apply-templates/>
  </xsl:invoke>
</xsl:template>
```

It is an error if a stylesheet contains more than one definition of a macro with the same name and same importance. An XSL processor may signal the error; if it does not signal the error, if must recover by choosing from amongst the definitions with highest importance the one that occurs last in the stylesheet.

Issue (macro-arg-syntax): The proposal used the same element for declaring macro arguments and for invoking them. Should these be separate elements and if so what should they be called?

2.8 Combining Stylesheets

XSL provides two mechanisms to combine stylesheets:

- an import mechanism that allows stylesheets to override each other, and
- an inclusion mechanism that allows stylesheets to be textually combined.

2.8.1 Stylesheet Import

An XSL stylesheet may contain `xsl:import` elements. All the `xsl:import` elements must occur at the beginning of the stylesheet. The `xsl:import` element has an href attribute whose value is the URI of a stylesheet to be imported. A relative URI is resolved relative to the base URI of the `xsl:import` element (see Section 2.4.2.2: Base URI).

```
<xsl:stylesheet xmlns:xsl="http://www.w3.org/TR/WD-xsl">
  <xsl:import href="article.xsl"/>
  <xsl:import href="bigfont.xsl"/>
  <xsl:attribute-set name="note-style">
    <xsl:attribute name="font-style">italic</xsl:attribute>
  </xsl:attribute-set>
</xsl:stylesheet>
```

Rules and definitions in the importing stylesheet are defined to be more important than rules and definitions in any imported stylesheets. Also rules and definitions in one *imported* stylesheet are defined to be more *important* than rules and definitions in previous imported stylesheets.

In general a more important rule or definition takes precedence over a less important rule or definition. This is defined in detail for each kind of rule and definition.

Issue (stylesheet-partition): Should there be an XSL defined element that can be used to divide a stylesheet into parts, each of which is treated as if it were separately imported for precedence purposes?

Issue (import-source): Provide a way for a stylesheet to import a stylesheet that is embedded in the document.

Issue (import-media): Should we provide media-dependent imports as in CSS?

Ed. Note: Say something about the case where the same stylesheet gets imported twice. This should be treated the same as importing a stylesheet with the same content but different URIs. What about import loops?

`xsl:apply-imports` processes the current node using only template rules that were imported into the stylesheet containing the current rule; the node is processed in the current rule's mode.

Ed. Note: Expand this.

2.8.2 Stylesheet Inclusion

An XSL stylesheet may include another XSL stylesheet using an `xsl:include` element. The `xsl:include` element has an href attribute whose value is the URI of a stylesheet to be included. A relative URI is resolved relative to the base URI of the `xsl:include` element (see Section 2.4.2.2: Base URI). The `xsl:include` element can occur as the child of the `xsl:stylesheet` element at any point after all `xsl:import` elements.

The inclusion works at the XML tree level. The resource located by the href attribute value is parsed as an XML document, and the children of the `xsl:stylesheet` element in this document replace the `xsl:include` element in the including document. Also any `xsl:import` elements in the included document are moved up in the including document to after any existing `xsl:import` elements in the including document. Unlike with `xsl:import`, the fact that rules or definitions are included does not affect the way they are processed.

Ed. Note: What happens when a stylesheet directly or indirectly includes itself?

2.8.3 Embedding Stylesheets

Normally an XSL stylesheet is a complete XML document with the `xsl:stylesheet` element as the document element. However an XSL stylesheet may also be embedded in another resource. Two forms of embedding are possible:

- the XSL stylesheet may be textually embedded in a non-XML resource, or
- the `xsl:stylesheet` element may occur in an XML document other than as the document element.

In the second case, the possibility arises of documents with inline style, that is documents that specify their own style. XSL does not define a specific mechanism for this. This is because this can be done by means of a general purpose mechanism for associating stylesheets with documents provided that:

the mechanism allows a part of a resource to be specified as the stylesheet, for example by using a URI with a fragment identifier, and

- the mechanism can itself can be embedded in the document, for example as a processing instruction.
- It is not in the scope of XSL to define such a mechanism.

NOTE: This is because the mechanism should be independent of any one stylesheet mechanism.

The xsl:stylesheet element may have an ID attribute that specifies a unique identifier.

NOTE: In order for such an attribute to be used with the id XPointer location term, it must actually be declared in the DTD as being an ID.

The following example shows how inline style can be accomplished using the xml-stylesheet processing instruction mechanism for associating a stylesheet with an XML document. The URI uses an XPointer in a fragment identifier to locate the xsl:stylesheet element.

```
<?xml version="1.0"?>
<?xml-stylesheet type="text/xsl" href="#id(style1)"?>
<!DOCTYPE doc SYSTEM "doc.dtd">
<doc>
<head>
<xsl:stylesheet xmlns:xsl="http://www.w3.org/TR/WD-xsl" id="style1">
<xsl:import href="doc.xsl"/>
<xsl:template match="id(foo)">
 <fo:block font-weight="bold"><xsl:apply-templates/></fo:block>
</xsl:template>
</xsl:stylesheet>
</head>
<body>
<para id="foo">
...
</para>
</body>
</doc>
```

NOTE: The type pseudo-attribute in the `xml-stylesheet` processing instruction identifies the stylesheet language, not the content type of the resource of which the stylesheet is a part.

2.9 Extensibility

This section will describe an extensibility mechanism for the tree construction process.

Issue (construct-extensibility): Should there be some extensibility mechanism for the tree construction process? If so, how should it work? Should it be language independent?

Chapter 3

Formatting

3.1 Introduction

The approach that we have taken in constructing this draft was to evaluate the requirements for print and online documents and established a target set of capabilities. This set of capabilities reflect the long-term goals of XSL.

In this draft we concentrated on documenting a subset of the formatting capability that addressed basic WP-level pagination. We expect to cover more sophisticated pagination and support for layout-driven documents in later drafts.

> **Ed. Note:** Because we are in the process of merging definitions to support the joint formatting model, we have not completed transfering all definitions from the previous draft.

3.2 Formatting Model

> **Ed. Note:** The formatting model portion of this specification is an exposition of a set of working notes developed by a sub-committee of XSL WG. The goals of this sub-committee have been (1) to develop input to the W3C Common Formatting Model and (2) to provide a semantic model in terms of which XSL can be described. The sub-committee has been integrating the CSS Box Model and the Area Semantics of XSL. We are distributing this work in progress, recognizing that the terminology used below is not fully integrated with the CSS or XSL terminology and that there are still technical issues in the XSL semantics needing resolution.

In XSL, one creates a number of formatting-objects that serve as inputs (or specifications) to a formatter. The formatter, by applying the formatting model, constructs a hierarchical arrangement of areas and spaces to produce the formatted result. This section describes that general model of spaces and areas, as well as how they interact with one another. The purpose is to present the fundamental semantics of formatting objects and properties, but not to specify individual flow objects. It should be seen as describing a series of constraints for conforming implementations, and not a prescribing any particular algorithm, e.g. for line breaking, letterspacing, hyphenation, or kerning.

3.2.1 Introduction

The formatting model is defined in terms of rectangular areas and spaces.

Areas reserve space and hold content.

Selected rectangular areas may have their own coordinate systems and may contain other rectangular areas.

Rectangular areas may be filled with other areas; when this happens the contained areas are placed in accordance with the writing-mode, a property of the containing area which controls the direction of placement of successive contained areas.

[**Ed. Note:** Further versions or extensions of the model may take into account non-rectangular areas.]

- A rectangular area is like a CSS box in that it has margins, borders, and padding, which are specified by properties of the formatting object that caused the creation of the area.

  [Ednote: We have not fully resolved technical differences between CSS's use of margins and XSL's use of display-space and inline-space. I have left the references to margins in this section, because I believe that these issues can be resolved and we will eventually need to describe handling of margins at those locations in the document.. However, the descriptions of the handling of inline-space and display-space is more accurate and more complete at this time.]

- Spaces reserve space before, after, or between areas and do not have content. They are used to make adjustments to the layout.

It is the responsibility of the formatter to manage inheritance and to specify the resultant properties when creating any area. This is necessary since this formatting model should be applicable to both XSL and CSS, which have differing inheritance strategies. It is therefore necessary for the formatter to derive certain properties when it creates (synthesizes) an area that has no directly related formatting object (such as the creation of line-areas within a block area).

3.2.2 Rectangular areas

There are four kinds of rectangular areas: area-containers, block-areas, line-areas, and inline-areas.

Area-containers may contain smaller area-containers. Alternatively, an area-container may be filled with a sequence of block-areas and display-spaces, which are stacked (placed sequentially and adjacent to one another, possibly separated by display-spaces) within the area-container in a direction determined by the writing-mode.

- Area-containers always have a writing-mode and set a coordinate system for all contained areas. The start-indent and end-indent of any block-area is measured from the area-container's corresponding edges, not from the edges of any intervening (nested) block-area.

  Area-containers may be placed at a specific positions within the containing area or may be attached to the inside of any edge of the containing area.

- Block-areas are filled with line-areas, display-spaces, and nested block-areas stacked (placed sequentially and adjacent to one another, possibly separated by display-spaces) in a direction determined by the writing-mode, or alternatively may consist of a graphic element.

  Block-areas should not be thought of as abstract entities which are "broken" across an area-container boundary; rather, at a container boundary a block-level formatting object may generate two (or more) block-areas.

  Block-areas are always stacked in the containing area.

- Line-areas are filled with inline-areas and inline-spaces in a direction determined by the writing-mode.

  Line-areas are always stacked (placed sequentially and adjacent to one another, possibly separated by display-spaces) in the containing block-area.

- An inline-area may contain other inline-areas. The lowest level inline-area commonly contains a single character glyph image (and is then called a glyph-area). An inline-area may have more complex content (e.g. an in-line mathematical expression).

  Inline-areas should not be thought of as abstract entities which are "broken" across a line boundary; rather, at a line boundary an inline formatting object may generate two (or more) inline-areas.

  Inline-areas are always stacked (placed sequentially and adjacent to one another, possibly separated by inline-spaces) in the containing area.

Rectangular areas have a number of common features. Each has a margin, border, and padding, defined as follows.

- A border is an open box surrounding the content of the area. A border is specified in terms of its color and of the thickness of each of its four sides. This thickness may be specified as a range with minimum, optimum, and maximum values.

- Padding is the open space between the inside of the border and the content of the area. It is specified by its thickness in each of the four directions.

- A margin is used to determine the open space reserved between the outside of the border of the rectangular area and those of other rectangular areas. It is specified by its thickness in each of the four directions, though only some of these may apply in determining the allocation-rectangle, described below.

Ed. Note: `<INSERT ILLUSTRATION—src="boxmodel.gif" alt="Box model dia-gram" vspace=0 hspace=50 border=0>`

By a rectangle we mean an open rectangle, consisting of four edges. This model identifies a number of specific rectangles:

- The content-rectangle of a rectangular area is the rectangle surrounding the area's content.
- The padding rectangle surrounds the area's padding. If the padding has 0 thickness, the padding rectangle is the same as the content-rectangle.
- The border rectangle surrounds the area's border. If the border has 0 width, the border rectangle is the same as the padding rectangle.
- The margin rectangle surrounds the area's margin. If the margin has 0 width, the margin rectangle is the same as the border rectangle.

All rectangular areas have properties which are either specified (explicitly) or derived. Margin, border and padding specifications are specified properties.

Among the properties of areas are the writing-mode. This determines the way glyphs are aligned (called the glyph-alignment-mode), and several directions used for rectangular area placement:

- block-progression-direction: the direction of progression of sequential block-areas within an area-container.
- line-progression-direction: the direction of progression of sequential line-areas within a block-area. This is usually the same as the block-progression-direction but may sometimes be opposite to the block-progression-direction.
- inline-progression-direction: the direction of progression of sequential inline-areas within a line-area. This is always perpendicular to the line-progression-direction.
- escapement-progression-direction: the direction of progression of sequential glyph-areas within an inline-area. This is usually the same as the inline-progression-direction but may sometimes be opposite to the inline-progression-direction.

Inline-areas have a designated position-point. We will define the descender-depth of a glyph-area to be how far it extends in the line-progression-direction from the position-point, and the ascender-height to be how far it extends in the opposite direction. Similar definitions may be made for more complex inline-areas.

The edges of any rectangle associated with a rectangular area are identified by their relative direction, based on the writing-mode.

- The edge occurring first in the block-progression-direction or the line-progression-direction (as applicable) and perpendicular to it is called the before-edge of the rectangle. The opposite edge is the after-edge.

- The edge occurring first in the inline-progression-direction or the escapement-progression-direction (as applicable) is called the start-edge of the rectangle. The opposite edge is called the end-edge.

In European writing systems, these are the "top" and "bottom" edges, and "left" and "right" edges, respectively, and "ascender-height" and "descender-depth" have their usual meanings.

Two rectangles associated to a rectangular area are of particular significance:

- The content-rectangle bounds the portion of the area in which the allocation-rectangles of smaller areas may appear. It is possible for marks associated with an area to be found outside the content-rectangle, but these are considered decoration and are deemed not to take up area.

- The allocation-rectangle bounds the portion of the area which is used to allocate space when placing the area inside a larger area. When we speak of an area's "size" we are normally referring to the dimensions of its allocation-rectangle.

  For area-containers the allocation-rectangle extends as far as the border rectangle in the block-progression-direction, and as far as the margin rectangle in the perpendicular direction.

  For all other rectangular areas, the allocation-rectangle extends to the margin rectangle in the inline-progression-direction. For block-areas it extends to the border rectangle in the line-progression-direction, and for line-areas and inline-areas, it extends only to the content-rectangle in that direction.

Ed. Note: <INSERT ILLUSTRATION—src="bcontent.gif"   alt="Block-level content & allocation rectangle" vspace=0 hspace=50 border=0>

Ed. Note: <INSERT ILLUSTRATION—src="lcontent.gif" alt="Inline-level content & allocation rectangle" vspace=0 hspace=50 border=0>

3.2.3 Display-spaces

Display-spaces are blank space assigned preceding and following line-areas and block-areas to control their placement. They are assigned either automatically by the formatter or as otherwise specified.

A display-space between two areas (block or line) is specified by a triple of values (minimum, optimum, maximum) which defines the limits of how the space may be transformed by later processes such as vertical justification. In the absence of further processing, the two areas will be separated by the optimum value, but such processing may reduce it as small as the specified minimum or stretch it as large as the specified maximum.

A display-space is thought of as having a before-edge and after-edge separated in the block-progression-direction or line-progression-direction by the display-space's value. A display-space value may be negative, which can cause areas to overlap.

When two or more display-spaces are adjacent, they shall be resolved into a single display-space whose minimum, optimum and maximum values are derived according to the space-resolution-rules, as described below. These depend on certain specified properties of the display-space, namely conditionality and precedence.

- Conditionality is a Boolean value which specifies whether the space persists at the beginning or end of an area-container. If true, the space is called a conditional-space and is always omitted if it appears at the before-edge or after-edge of the content-rectangle of an area-container; in this case any immediately succeeding conditional-spaces are also omitted.
- Precedence has a value which is either an integer or the special token "force". A space with a precedence value of "force" is called a forcing space.

Space-resolution-rules. When several spaces are assigned to be adjacent, they are resolved into a single space as follows:

1. At the beginning or end of an area-container, any conditional-spaces are omitted if this has not already been done.
2. Then, if any space is forcing, the resolved space is taken to be the sum of all the forcing spaces, and all non-forcing spaces are suppressed.
3. If all spaces are non-forcing, then the eligible spaces shall be those with the maximum precedence, and among these, the space or spaces having the greatest optimum value. All other spaces are suppressed. The resolved space is taken to have the same optimum value as the eligible spaces; its minimum value shall be the greatest of the minimum values of the eligible spaces, and its maximum value shall be the least of the maximum values.

A display-space at the before-edge or after-edge of the content-rectangle of a block-area is combined with the padding of the block-area in that direction according to the space-resolution-rules, except that the resolved display-space is never resolved to be smaller than the padding.

> **Ed. Note:** The border or padding associated with a rectangular area may be specified as conditional. For purposes of conditionality, if the border or padding of the area are non-zero and not omitted, then the initial space within the area's content rectangle is not at the beginning of an area container (and so is not omitted in step 1).

3.2.4 Inline-spaces

Inline-spaces are blank space assigned preceding and following inline-areas. They are assigned either automatically by the formatter (e.g. for word spacing, letterspacing, or kerning) or as otherwise specified.

An inline-space is specified by a triple of values (minimum, optimum, maximum) which defines the limits of how the space may be transformed by later processes such as justification. It separates inline-areas in a direct analogy to the way display-space separates block-areas.

An inline-space is thought of as having a start-edge and end-edge, separated in the inline-progression-direction by the inline-space's value. An inline-space value may be negative, which can cause inline-areas to overlap.

Inline-spaces have conditionality and precedence. Conditional inline-spaces are omitted at the start and end of a line-area. When multiple inline-spaces are assigned to be adjacent, they are resolved in accordance with the space-resolution-rules.

> **Ed. Note:** Most formatters have built-in algorithms for the handling of word-spacing, letter-spacing, kerning, and combinations thereof; although this model describes these features using inline-spaces and space-resolution-rules, it is not the intent of this standard to demand replacement of the formatter's built-in algorithms.

3.2.5 Area containers

An area-container defines a coordinate system for its content, which may be oriented differently from that of its containing area.

The block-progression-direction of an area-container is derived from its coordinate system and its writing-mode, and controls the orientation and placement of block-areas in the area-container.

The allocation-rectangle of an area-container has a fixed size in the direction perpendicular to its block-progression-direction, and may have a fixed size in the block-progression-direction, or may grow to accommodate its content.

Area-containers may directly contain smaller area-containers, or alternatively may be filled with block-areas. Area-containers may be directly contained in larger area-containers, block-areas, or inline-areas, or may be uncontained (e.g. a page area).

3.2.6 Block-areas

A block-area's margins, borders, and padding are specified by the formatter based on the properties of its generating flow object.

A block-area's writing-mode is specified by the formatter (though the formatter may choose to derive the value from its containing area). This determines its line-progression-direction, which controls the orientation and placement of line-areas in its content-rectangle, and its inline-progression-direction, which is used to determine the direction of writing within contained line-areas.

Block-areas also have a specified nominal-font (a fully qualified font name and font size), which is used by the formatter to establish a default font for the block-area's directly contained line-areas and block-areas, but may be overridden. Other properties include line-height (the nominal distance between the before-edges of successive line-areas), minimum-leading (the minimum space allowed between line-areas), and space-before and space-after specifications (which may be identified with the specifications for before- and after-margins).

A derived property of a block-area is its nominal-glyph-height, which is the distance from the maximum ascender-height to the maximum descender depth of the glyph-areas of the nominal-font. This is a property of the nominal-font and is not dependent on which glyphs are actually present in the block-area.

The allocation-rectangle of a block-area has fixed size in the inline-progression-direction, and varies in the line-progression-direction to accommodate its content, though this may not grow outside the content-rectangle of its containing area. (The overflow property does allow the content to exceed the allocation-rectangle under limited circumstances. The overflowing data is considered decoration and is not considered as part of the layout. Overflowing data may be clipped or may overprint content in other areas.) A block-area consisting of a graphic element has fixed size in both directions.

A block-area may directly contain line-areas, display-spaces, and nested block-areas, or may consist of a graphic element. Block-areas may be directly contained in area-containers and higher-level block-areas.

3.2.7 Line-areas

There is no formatting-object that directly corresponds to a line-area. Thus, line-areas are always created by the formatter. A line-area's margins, borders, and padding are derived by the formatter from the settings on the containing area.

A line-area also derives its inline-progression-direction from its containing block-area, and this is used to determine the direction of writing within a line. It also derives its line-height and minimum-leading properties, as well as its nominal-font, which is used to derive its nominal-glyph-height.

The allocation-rectangle of a line is determined by the presence or absence of the minimum-leading property: if absent, the allocation-rectangle is the nominal-requested-line-rectangle; if present, it is the maximum-line-rectangle, as described below.

The nominal-requested-line-rectangle for a line-area is the rectangle bounded in the inline-progression-direction by the content-rectangle of the containing block-area, as modified by typographic properties such as indents, and in the perpendicular direction by its nominal-glyph-height. It has the same height for each line in a block-area.

The maximum-line-rectangle for a line has the same length as the nominal-requested-line-rectangle in the inline-progression-direction. In the perpendicular direction it is bounded by the maximum ascender-height and the maximum descender-depth for the actual fonts and inline-areas placed on the line, as raised and lowered by vertical-align and other adjustments perpendicular to the inline-progression-direction. Its height may vary depending on the contents of the line-area.

Ed. Note: <INSERT ILLUSTRATION—src="linerect.gif" alt="Nominal and Maximum line rectangles" vspace=0 hspace=50 border=0>

The nominal-font is always deemed to occur on a line, and thus the maximum-line-rectangle always contains the nominal-requested-line-rectangle.

Inline-areas are placed within a line-area relative to a placement-point . This varies during the placement process, but initially the placement-point is a point on the start-edge of its content-rectangle, separated from the before-edge of the nominal-requested-line-rectangle by a distance equal to the ascender-height for the nominal-font.

Line-areas may directly contain inline-areas and inline-spaces. They may be directly contained in block-areas.

Ed. Note: We may require special-casing rules for the maximum line rectangle in cases such as "accented" strings in mathematics, or ruby or non-spacing superiors.

3.2.8 Inline-areas

The most common inline-area is a glyph-area, which contains the representation for a character in a particular font. Other examples of inline-areas might include portions of inline mathematical expressions.

Inline-areas have margins, borders, and padding, specified by the formatter. (The margins before and after an inline-area are disregarded in determining the size of its allocation-rectangle. However, margins at the start-edge and end-edge are incorporated into the allocation-rectangle.)

The allocation-rectangle for an inline-area has a fixed size in both dimensions, though this may be specified as a range within which the size may be modified by further processes such as justification. An inline-area also has a font, which is derived from the containing area (if not explicitly set on the inline-area).

Each inline-area has a designated position-point on one of the edges of its allocation-rectangle (typically the start-edge). On the opposite edge of the allocation-rectangle there is another point called the escapement-point, and the vector from the position-point to the escapement-point is called the escapement-vector.

The position-point and escapement-point are assigned according to the writing-system in use (e.g. the glyph baseline in European languages) and the current escapement-progression-direction in effect for bidirectional text. These points may be futher adjusted in the case of mixed-language formatting involving different glyph-alignment-modes.

A glyph-area is atomic and may contain no other areas. An inline-area may be atomic and contain no other areas, or may be non-atomic and contain an area-container (such as for an inline-graphic), a block-area or other inline-areas. Inline-areas may be directly contained only in line-areas or in other inline-areas.

3.2.9 Inline-area placement within a line-area

The formatter constructs a series of inline-areas and assigns these to line-areas according to its line-breaking algorithm.

Inline-areas assigned to a line-area are placed in the line-area in their display order (which may be different from the logical order, when writing-systems are mixed).

Before an inline-area is placed, the placement-point of the line-area may be adjusted by shifts perpendicular to the inline-progression-direction (e.g. for subscript and superscript, or to allow for glyphs with a different natural alignment from the line-area's glyph-alignment mode).

Each inline-area is oriented so that the direction of its escapement-vector matches the escapement-progression-direction, and is placed so that its position-point matches the current placement-point of the line-area. The escapement-point of the inline-area then becomes the new placement-point.

Each inline-space is placed so that its start-edge intersects the current placement-point, and the placement-point is translated in the inline-progression-direction, to the end-edge of the inline-space. Adjacent spaces are combined according to the space-resolution-rules. A conditional-space is not placed if it is at the start-edge of the content-rectangle of a line-area, but may be placed if it follows a non-conditional-space there. Similarly a conditional-space is not placed if it is at the end of a line-area, but may be placed if it precedes a non-conditional-space there.

> **Ed. Note:** In bidirectional text, the display order is generated according to the basic algorithm for display of bidirectional text in the Unicode Standard, version 2.1.

3.2.10 Line-area placement within a block-area

Preceding and following each line-area assigned to a block-area, the formatter assigns display-spaces, whose conditionality and precedence are determined by the generating flow object.

The values of these display-spaces are determined by the presence or absence of the minimum-leading property. If minimum-leading is present then the value of each is equal to half the value of minimum-leading. Otherwise it is equal to half of the difference between the line-height and nominal-glyph-height, as derived from the containing block-area (if not set explicitly on the inline-area).

Each display-space is placed so that its before-edge coincides with the after-edge of the allocation-rectangle of the previous block-area or line-area. Adjacent spaces are combined according to the space-resolution-rules. A conditional-space is not placed if it is at the before-edge of the content-rectangle of an area-container, but may be placed if it follows a non-conditional-space there. Similarly a conditional-space is not placed at the after-edge, but may be placed if it precedes a non-conditional-space there.

Each line-area is placed so that the before-edge of its allocation-rectangle matches the after-edge of the previous display-space, line-area, or block-area, or failing these, the before-edge of the content-rectangle of its containing block-area. The start-edge and end-edges of the allocation-rectangle are placed to coincide with corresponding edges of the content-rectangle of the containing block-area.

> **Ed. Note:** Future versions or extensions of the model may take into account intrusions and runaround text.

3.2.11 Block-area placement

Preceding and following each block-area assigned to an area-container, or nested inside another block-area, the formatter assigns display-spaces, whose height, conditionality and precedence are determined in accordance with its space-before and space-after properties, and by other properties of the generating flow object.

Each display-space is placed so that its before-edge coincides with the after-edge of the allocation-rectangle of the previous block-area or line-area. Adjacent spaces are combined according to the space-resolution-rules. A conditional-space is not placed if it is at the before-edge of the content-rectangle of an area-container, but may be placed if it follows a non-conditional-space there, and similarly for the after-edge.

Each block-area is placed so that the before-edge of its allocation-rectangle matches the after-edge of the previous display-space, line-area, or block-area, or failing that, the before-edge of the content-rectangle of the containing area-container or block-area.

The start-edge and end-edges of its allocation-rectangle are placed to coincide with the corresponding edges of the content-rectangle of the containing block-area or area-container.

In no case is the space between block-areas affected by the display-spaces contained in those block-areas, or in particular by their specified values of line-height.

Ed. Note: NOTE: We recognize that this requirement goes too far and plan to change it to allow the merging of spaces from nested block-areas, while still not allowing merging between a space-after from a block with the half-leading before the first line of the next block.

3.3 Formatting Objects Summary

basic-page-sequence

This object describes the general layout or layout sequencing for web page (both print and online).

block

A block formatting object allows the formatter to create a block-level area that contains textlines.

character

The character formatting object is used when one needs to explicitly override a specific character or array of characters with a specific glyph.

display-graphic

Creates a block-level area that contains a graphic.

display-link

A link that produces a block-level area.

display-rule

Produces a block-level rule (line).

display-sequence

A display-sequence is used to group block-level flow objects and to assign inherited properties to be shared across them.

inline-graphic

Creates a inline area that contains a graphic.

inline-link

A link that produces an inline area.

inline-rule

Produces a inline rule (line).

inline-sequence

An inline-sequence is used to group inline flow objects and to assign inherited properties to be shared across them.

link-end-locator

Represents a target for link.

list-block

Creates a block-level area containing a list.

list-item

A list-item flow object contains the label and the body of each item; it may be used for overriding and modifying some of the list's properties on a case by case basis.

list-item-body

The item-body flow object holds the components (usually blocks) for a list item. It controls styling defaults for the body, the spacing between lines and between paras within the list item, break precedences for line and paragraphs within the list item.

list-item-label

A list-item-label is used to either enumerate, identify or adorn the list-item's body.

page-number

This object is used to instruct the formatter to construct and present a page-number.

queue

A queue is used to gather content flow objects to be assigned to (placed into) a given area or set of chained-areas.

simple-page-master

A simple-page-master formatting object defines the layout of a page area. Masters may be repeated in accordance with the page-sequence specification.

3.4 Formatting Objects

3.4.1 fo:basic-page-sequence

3.4.1.1 Purpose

This object describes the general layout or layout sequencing for web page (both print and online).

3.4.1.2 Description

A basic-page-sequence holds:

- a number of child simple-page-masters that define the layouts to be used for this sequence.
- a number of child queues which hold the content to be placed in this sequence.

NOTE: A document can contain multiple basic-page-sequences. For example, each chapter of a document could be a separate basic-page-sequence; this would allow the chapter title within a header or footer.

3.4.1.3 Properties

- id : Section 3.5.68: id
- first-page-master : Section 3.5.42: first-page-master

3.4.2 fo:block

3.4.2.1 Purpose

A block formatting object allows the formatter to create a block-level area that contains textlines.

3.4.2.2 Description

This object is commonly used for formatting paragraphs, titles, headlines, figure and table captions, etc. It normally specifies a rectangular area that occupies the width of the containing area and a height that is determined by the amount of text that the block contains. A block may specify separation between it and a preceding block-level object or subsequent block-level object as well as unique indents on the start of the first textline of the block and end of the last textline of the block.

A block directly contains its children, which may be a mixture of inline or block-level formatting objects:

- Inline child formatting objects within a block are formatted to produce one or more textline areas. Multiple inline objects may be placed successively into a single textline. Inline objects may (or may not) be split across two or more textlines if necessary (and if allowed to split) if the inline does not fit in the remaining space in the textline.
- Block-level child formatting objects within a block implicitly specify line-breaks before and after the block-level object. Each child block-level produces a single area which is treated by the formatter of the block as if it were a textline area. These areas shall be added to the resulting sequence of areas within the block.

NOTE: This specifies that users may nest a block inside another block. When this happens the outer block does not end before the nested block, it is simply suspended. The normal mid-block quadding and indents apply to the last textline prior to the nested block's area. Similarly, the outer block resumes after the nested block without a new first-textline indent.

NOTE: Typically, a break implies that a new textline is to be started. The shift-direction for inline areas in the block is the reverse of the line-progression-direction of the block.

3.4.2.3 Properties

- background-attachment : Section 3.5.4: background-attachment
- background-color : Section 3.5.5: background-color
- background-image : Section 3.5.6: background-image
- background-position : Section 3.5.7: background-position
- background-repeat : Section 3.5.8: background-repeat
- border-color-top : Section 3.5.18: border-color-top
- border-color-bottom : Section 3.5.13: border-color-bottom
- border-color-left : Section 3.5.15: border-color-left
- border-sscolor-right : Section 3.5.16: border-color-right
- border-color-before : Section 3.5.12: border-color-before
- border-color-after : Section 3.5.11: border-color-after
- border-color-start : Section 3.5.17: border-color-start
- border-color-end : Section 3.5.14: border-color-end
- border-width-top : Section 3.5.26: border-width-top
- border-width-bottom : Section 3.5.21: border-width-bottom
- border-width-left : Section 3.5.23: border-width-left
- border-width-right : Section 3.5.24: border-width-right
- border-width-before : Section 3.5.20: border-width-before
- border-width-after : Section 3.5.19: border-width-after
- border-width-start : Section 3.5.25: border-width-start
- border-width-end : Section 3.5.22: border-width-end
- break-before : Section 3.5.28: break-before
- break-after : Section 3.5.27: break-after
- font-family : Section 3.5.43: font-family
- system-font : Section 3.5.135: system-font
- font-size : Section 3.5.44: font-size
- font-size-adjust : Section 3.5.45: font-size-adjust
- font-stretch : Section 3.5.46: font-stretch

- font-style : Section 3.5.47: font-style
- font-variant : Section 3.5.48: font-variant
- font-weight : Section 3.5.49: font-weight
- glyph-alignment-mode : Section 3.5.54: glyph-alignment-mode
- hyphenation-keep : Section 3.5.64: hyphenation-keep
- id : Section 3.5.68: id
- text-indent : Section 3.5.138: text-indent
- end-indent : Section 3.5.34: end-indent
- start-indent : Section 3.5.130: start-indent
- keep : Section 3.5.73: keep
- orphans : Section 3.5.98: orphans
- widows : Section 3.5.141: widows
- keep-with-next : Section 3.5.74: keep-with-next
- keep-with-previous : Section 3.5.75: keep-with-previous
- language : Section 3.5.78: language
- letter-spacing : Section 3.5.81: letter-spacing
- letter-spacing-limit : Section 3.5.82: letter-spacing-limit
- line-height : Section 3.5.84: line-height
- line-height-option : Section 3.5.85: line-height-option
- min-leading : Section 3.5.94: min-leading
- min-post-line-spacing : Section 3.5.95: min-post-line-spacing
- min-pre-line-spacing : Section 3.5.96: min-pre-line-spacing
- line-spacing-precedence : Section 3.5.87: line-spacing-precedence
- padding-top : Section 3.5.107: padding-top
- padding-bottom : Section 3.5.102: padding-bottom
- padding-left : Section 3.5.104: padding-left
- padding-right : Section 3.5.105: padding-right
- padding-before : Section 3.5.101: padding-before
- padding-after : Section 3.5.100: padding-after

- padding-start : Section 3.5.106: padding-start
- padding-end : Section 3.5.103: padding-end
- space-after : Section 3.5.125: space-after
- space-before : Section 3.5.126: space-before
- text-align : Section 3.5.136: text-align
- text-align-last : Section 3.5.137: text-align-last
- asis-truncate-indicator : Section 3.5.1: asis-truncate-indicator
- asis-wrap-indent : Section 3.5.2: asis-wrap-indent
- asis-wrap-indicator : Section 3.5.3: asis-wrap-indicator
- expand-tabs : Section 3.5.41: expand-tabs
- ignore-record-end : Section 3.5.69: ignore-record-end
- wrap-option : Section 3.5.145: wrap-option
- writing-mode : Section 3.5.146: writing-mode

3.4.3 fo:character

3.4.3.1 Purpose

The character formatting object is used when one needs to explicitly override a specific character or array of characters with a specific glyph.

3.4.3.2 Description

When the result tree is interpreted as a tree of formatting objects, a character in the result tree is treated as if it were an empty element of type fo:character with a char attribute equal to the character.

3.4.3.3 Properties

- background-attachment : Section 3.5.4: background-attachment
- background-color : Section 3.5.5: background-color
- background-image : Section 3.5.6: background-image
- background-position : Section 3.5.7: background-position
- background-repeat : Section 3.5.8: background-repeat
- border-color-top : Section 3.5.18: border-color-top
- border-color-bottom : Section 3.5.13: border-color-bottom

- border-color-left : Section 3.5.15: border-color-left
- border-color-right : Section 3.5.16: border-color-right
- border-color-before : Section 3.5.12: border-color-before
- border-color-after : Section 3.5.11: border-color-after
- border-color-start : Section 3.5.17: border-color-start
- border-color-end : Section 3.5.14: border-color-end
- border-width-top : Section 3.5.26: border-width-top
- border-width-bottom : Section 3.5.21: border-width-bottom
- border-width-left : Section 3.5.23: border-width-left
- border-width-right : Section 3.5.24: border-width-right
- border-width-before : Section 3.5.20: border-width-before
- border-width-after : Section 3.5.19: border-width-after
- border-width-start : Section 3.5.25: border-width-start
- border-width-end : Section 3.5.22: border-width-end
- character : Section 3.5.29: character
- color : Section 3.5.30: color
- font-family : Section 3.5.43: font-family
- system-font : Section 3.5.135: system-font
- font-size : Section 3.5.44: font-size
- font-size-adjust : Section 3.5.45: font-size-adjust
- font-stretch : Section 3.5.46: font-stretch
- font-style : Section 3.5.47: font-style
- font-variant : Section 3.5.48: font-variant
- font-weight : Section 3.5.49: font-weight
- glyph-id : Section 3.5.55: glyph-id
- hyphenate : Section 3.5.62: hyphenate
- hyphenation-char : Section 3.5.63: hyphenation-char
- hyphenation-ladder-count : Section 3.5.65: hyphenation-ladder-count
- hyphenation-push-char-count : Section 3.5.66: hyphenation-push-char-count

- hyphenation-remain-char-count : Section 3.5.67: hyphenation-remain-char-count
- id : Section 3.5.68: id
- inhibit-line-breaks : Section 3.5.71: inhibit-line-breaks
- kern : Section 3.5.76: kern
- kern-mode : Section 3.5.77: kern-mode
- language : Section 3.5.78: language
- letter-spacing : Section 3.5.81: letter-spacing
- ligature : Section 3.5.83: ligature
- padding-top : Section 3.5.107: padding-top
- padding-bottom : Section 3.5.102: padding-bottom
- padding-left : Section 3.5.104: padding-left
- padding-right : Section 3.5.105: padding-right
- padding-before : Section 3.5.101: padding-before
- padding-after : Section 3.5.100: padding-after
- padding-start : Section 3.5.106: padding-start
- padding-end : Section 3.5.103: padding-end
- vertical-align : Section 3.5.140: vertical-align
- escapement-space-start : Section 3.5.40: escapement-space-start
- text-shadow : Section 3.5.139: text-shadow
- input-whitespace-treatment : Section 3.5.72: input-whitespace-treatment
- word-spacing : Section 3.5.143: word-spacing
- word-spacing-limit : Section 3.5.144: word-spacing-limit
- writing-mode : Section 3.5.146: writing-mode

3.4.4 fo:display-graphic

3.4.4.1 Purpose

Creates a block-level area that contains a graphic.

3.4.4.2 Description

This object creates a block-level area that contains a graphic.

3.4.4.3 Properties

- background-attachment : Section 3.5.4: background-attachment
- background-color : Section 3.5.5: background-color
- background-image : Section 3.5.6: background-image
- background-position : Section 3.5.7: background-position
- background-repeat : Section 3.5.8: background-repeat
- border-color-top : Section 3.5.18: border-color-top
- border-color-bottom : Section 3.5.13: border-color-bottom
- border-color-left : Section 3.5.15: border-color-left
- border-color-right : Section 3.5.16: border-color-right
- border-color-before : Section 3.5.12: border-color-before
- border-color-after : Section 3.5.11: border-color-after
- border-color-start : Section 3.5.17: border-color-start
- border-color-end : Section 3.5.14: border-color-end
- border-width-top : Section 3.5.26: border-width-top
- border-width-bottom : Section 3.5.21: border-width-bottom
- border-width-left : Section 3.5.23: border-width-left
- border-width-right : Section 3.5.24: border-width-right
- border-width-before : Section 3.5.20: border-width-before
- border-width-after : Section 3.5.19: border-width-after
- border-width-start : Section 3.5.25: border-width-start
- border-width-end : Section 3.5.22: border-width-end
- break-before : Section 3.5.28: break-before
- break-after : Section 3.5.27: break-after
- color : Section 3.5.30: color
- max-height : Section 3.5.91: max-height
- id : Section 3.5.68: id
- image : Section 3.5.70: image
- end-indent : Section 3.5.34: end-indent

- start-indent : Section 3.5.130: start-indent
- inhibit-line-breaks : Section 3.5.71: inhibit-line-breaks
- keep : Section 3.5.73: keep
- keep-with-next : Section 3.5.74: keep-with-next
- keep-with-previous : Section 3.5.75: keep-with-previous
- padding-top : Section 3.5.107: padding-top
- padding-bottom : Section 3.5.102: padding-bottom
- padding-left : Section 3.5.104: padding-left
- padding-right : Section 3.5.105: padding-right.
- padding-before : Section 3.5.101: padding-before
- padding-after : Section 3.5.100: padding-after
- padding-start : Section 3.5.106: padding-start
- padding-end : Section 3.5.103: padding-end
- position-point : Section 3.5.116: position-point
- scale-graphic : Section 3.5.122: scale-graphic
- space-after : Section 3.5.125: space-after
- space-before : Section 3.5.126: space-before
- max-width : Section 3.5.92: max-width
- writing-mode : Section 3.5.146: writing-mode

3.4.5 fo:display-link

3.4.5.1 Purpose

A link that produces a block-level area.

3.4.5.2 Description

This object represents a link that produces a block-level area. The children of this object will be the "hot spot" for the activation of the link.

3.4.5.3 Properties

- background-attachment : Section 3.5.4: background-attachment
- background-color : Section 3.5.5: background-color

- background-image : Section 3.5.6: background-image
- background-position : Section 3.5.7: background-position
- background-repeat : Section 3.5.8: background-repeat
- border-color-top : Section 3.5.18: border-color-top
- border-color-bottom : Section 3.5.13: border-color-bottom
- border-color-left : Section 3.5.15: border-color-left
- border-color-right : Section 3.5.16: border-color-right
- border-color-before : Section 3.5.12: border-color-before
- border-color-after : Section 3.5.11: border-color-after
- border-color-start : Section 3.5.17: border-color-start
- border-color-end : Section 3.5.14: border-color-end
- border-width-top : Section 3.5.26: border-width-top
- border-width-bottom : Section 3.5.21: border-width-bottom
- border-width-left : Section 3.5.23: border-width-left
- border-width-right : Section 3.5.24: border-width-right
- border-width-before : Section 3.5.20: border-width-before
- border-width-after : Section 3.5.19: border-width-after
- border-width-start : Section 3.5.25: border-width-start
- border-width-end : Section 3.5.22: border-width-end
- destination : Section 3.5.33: destination
- padding-top : Section 3.5.107: padding-top
- padding-bottom : Section 3.5.102: padding-bottom
- padding-left : Section 3.5.104: padding-left
- padding-right : Section 3.5.105: padding-right
- padding-before : Section 3.5.101: padding-before
- padding-after : Section 3.5.100: padding-after
- padding-start : Section 3.5.106: padding-start
- padding-end : Section 3.5.103: padding-end

3.4.6 fo:display-rule

3.4.6.1 Purpose

Produces a block-level rule (line).

3.4.6.2 Description

This object represents a block-level rule. It creates a line according to the properties that produces a block-level area.

3.4.6.3 Properties

- background-attachment : Section 3.5.4: background-attachment
- background-color : Section 3.5.5: background-color
- background-image : Section 3.5.6: background-image
- background-position : Section 3.5.7: background-position
- background-repeat : Section 3.5.8: background-repeat
- border-color-top : Section 3.5.18: border-color-top
- border-color-bottom : Section 3.5.13: border-color-bottom
- border-color-left : Section 3.5.15: border-color-left
- border-color-right : Section 3.5.16: border-color-right
- border-color-before : Section 3.5.12: border-color-before
- border-color-after : Section 3.5.11: border-color-after
- border-color-start : Section 3.5.17: border-color-start
- border-color-end : Section 3.5.14: border-color-end
- border-width-top : Section 3.5.26: border-width-top
- border-width-bottom : Section 3.5.21: border-width-bottom
- border-width-left : Section 3.5.23: border-width-left
- border-width-right : Section 3.5.24: border-width-right
- border-width-before : Section 3.5.20: border-width-before
- border-width-after : Section 3.5.19: border-width-after
- border-width-start : Section 3.5.25: border-width-start
- border-width-end : Section 3.5.22: border-width-end

- break-before : Section 3.5.28: break-before
- break-after : Section 3.5.27: break-after
- color : Section 3.5.30: color
- line-offset : Section 3.5.86: line-offset
- line-thickness : Section 3.5.88: line-thickness
- id : Section 3.5.68: id
- end-indent : Section 3.5.34: end-indent
- start-indent : Section 3.5.130: start-indent
- inhibit-line-breaks : Section 3.5.71: inhibit-line-breaks
- keep : Section 3.5.73: keep
- keep-with-next : Section 3.5.74: keep-with-next
- keep-with-previous : Section 3.5.75: keep-with-previous
- length : Section 3.5.80: length
- orientation : Section 3.5.97: orientation
- padding-top : Section 3.5.107: padding-top
- padding-bottom : Section 3.5.102: padding-bottom
- padding-left : Section 3.5.104: padding-left
- padding-right : Section 3.5.105: padding-right
- padding-before : Section 3.5.101: padding-before
- padding-after : Section 3.5.100: padding-after
- padding-start : Section 3.5.106: padding-start
- padding-end : Section 3.5.103: padding-end
- vertical-align : Section 3.5.140: vertical-align
- space-after : Section 3.5.125: space-after
- space-before : Section 3.5.126: space-before
- writing-mode : Section 3.5.146: writing-mode

3.4.7 fo:display-sequence

3.4.7.1 Purpose

A display-sequence is used to group block-level flow objects and to assign inherited properties to be shared across them.

3.4.7.2 Description

A display-sequence formatting object is formatted to produce the series of the block-level areas produced by each of its children. This object must contain only block-level flow objects and holds its content as children.

A display-sequence has no applicable properties.

3.4.7.3 Properties

- id : Section 3.5.68: id

3.4.8 fo:inline-graphic

3.4.8.1 Purpose

Creates a inline area that contains a graphic.

3.4.8.2 Description

This object creates an inline area that contains a graphic.

3.4.8.3 Properties

- background-attachment : Section 3.5.4: background-attachment
- background-color : Section 3.5.5: background-color
- background-image : Section 3.5.6: background-image
- background-position : Section 3.5.7: background-position
- background-repeat : Section 3.5.8: background-repeat
- border-color-top : Section 3.5.18: border-color-top
- border-color-bottom : Section 3.5.13: border-color-bottom
- border-color-left : Section 3.5.15: border-color-left
- border-color-right : Section 3.5.16: border-color-right

- border-color-before : Section 3.5.12: border-color-before
- border-color-after : Section 3.5.11: border-color-after
- border-color-start : Section 3.5.17: border-color-start
- border-color-end : Section 3.5.14: border-color-end
- border-width-top : Section 3.5.26: border-width-top
- border-width-bottom : Section 3.5.21: border-width-bottom
- border-width-left : Section 3.5.23: border-width-left
- border-width-right : Section 3.5.24: border-width-right
- border-width-before : Section 3.5.20: border-width-before
- border-width-after : Section 3.5.19: border-width-after
- border-width-start : Section 3.5.25: border-width-start
- border-width-end : Section 3.5.22: border-width-end
- color : Section 3.5.30: color
- max-height : Section 3.5.91: max-height
- id : Section 3.5.68: id
- image : Section 3.5.70: image
- end-indent : Section 3.5.34: end-indent
- start-indent : Section 3.5.130: start-indent
- inhibit-line-breaks : Section 3.5.71: inhibit-line-breaks
- keep : Section 3.5.73: keep
- keep-with-next : Section 3.5.74: keep-with-next
- keep-with-previous : Section 3.5.75: keep-with-previous
- padding-top : Section 3.5.107: padding-top
- padding-bottom : Section 3.5.102: padding-bottom
- padding-left : Section 3.5.104: padding-left
- padding-right : Section 3.5.105: padding-right
- padding-before : Section 3.5.101: padding-before
- padding-after : Section 3.5.100: padding-after
- padding-start : Section 3.5.106: padding-start

- padding-end : Section 3.5.103: padding-end
- vertical-align : Section 3.5.140: vertical-align
- scale-graphic : Section 3.5.122: scale-graphic
- space-end : Section 3.5.128: space-end
- space-start : Section 3.5.129: space-start
- max-width : Section 3.5.92: max-width
- writing-mode : Section 3.5.146: writing-mode

3.4.9 fo:inline-link

3.4.9.1 Purpose

A link that produces an inline area.

3.4.9.2 Description

This object represents a link that produces a inline area. The children of this object will be the "hot spot" for the activation of the link.

3.4.9.3 Properties

- background-attachment : Section 3.5.4: background-attachment
- background-color : Section 3.5.5: background-color
- background-image : Section 3.5.6: background-image
- background-position : Section 3.5.7: background-position
- background-repeat : Section 3.5.8: background-repeat
- border-color-top : Section 3.5.18: border-color-top
- border-color-bottom : Section 3.5.13: border-color-bottom
- border-color-left : Section 3.5.15: border-color-left
- border-color-right : Section 3.5.16: border-color-right
- border-color-before : Section 3.5.12: border-color-before
- border-color-after : Section 3.5.11: border-color-after
- border-color-start : Section 3.5.17: border-color-start
- border-color-end : Section 3.5.14: border-color-end

- border-width-top : Section 3.5.26: border-width-top
- border-width-bottom : Section 3.5.21: border-width-bottom
- border-width-left : Section 3.5.23: border-width-left
- border-width-right : Section 3.5.24: border-width-right
- border-width-before : Section 3.5.20: border-width-before
- border-width-after : Section 3.5.19: border-width-after
- border-width-start : Section 3.5.25: border-width-start
- border-width-end : Section 3.5.22: border-width-end
- destination : Section 3.5.33: destination
- padding-top : Section 3.5.107: padding-top
- padding-bottom : Section 3.5.102: padding-bottom
- padding-left : Section 3.5.104: padding-left
- padding-right : Section 3.5.105: padding-right
- padding-before : Section 3.5.101: padding-before
- padding-after : Section 3.5.100: padding-after
- padding-start : Section 3.5.106: padding-start
- padding-end : Section 3.5.103: padding-end

3.4.10 fo:inline-rule

3.4.10.1 Purpose

Produces a inline rule (line).

3.4.10.2 Description

This object represents a inline rule. It creates a line according to the properties that produces a inline area.

3.4.10.3 Properties

- background-attachment : Section 3.5.4: background-attachment
- background-color : Section 3.5.5: background-color
- background-image : Section 3.5.6: background-image

- background-position : Section 3.5.7: background-position
- background-repeat : Section 3.5.8: background-repeat
- border-color-top : Section 3.5.18: border-color-top
- border-color-bottom : Section 3.5.13: border-color-bottom
- border-color-left : Section 3.5.15: border-color-left
- border-color-right : Section 3.5.16: border-color-right
- border-color-before : Section 3.5.12: border-color-before
- border-color-after : Section 3.5.11: border-color-after
- border-color-start : Section 3.5.17: border-color-start
- border-color-end : Section 3.5.14: border-color-end
- border-width-top : Section 3.5.26: border-width-top
- border-width-bottom : Section 3.5.21: border-width-bottom
- border-width-left : Section 3.5.23: border-width-left
- border-width-right : Section 3.5.24: border-width-right
- border-width-before : Section 3.5.20: border-width-before
- border-width-after : Section 3.5.19: border-width-after
- border-width-start : Section 3.5.25: border-width-start
- border-width-end : Section 3.5.22: border-width-end
- color : Section 3.5.30: color
- line-offset : Section 3.5.86: line-offset
- line-thickness : Section 3.5.88: line-thickness
- id : Section 3.5.68: id
- end-indent : Section 3.5.34: end-indent
- start-indent : Section 3.5.130: start-indent
- inhibit-line-breaks : Section 3.5.71: inhibit-line-breaks
- keep : Section 3.5.73: keep
- keep-with-next : Section 3.5.74: keep-with-next
- keep-with-previous : Section 3.5.75: keep-with-previous
- length : Section 3.5.80: length

- orientation : Section 3.5.97: orientation
- padding-top : Section 3.5.107: padding-top
- padding-bottom : Section 3.5.102: padding-bottom
- padding-left : Section 3.5.104: padding-left
- padding-right : Section 3.5.105: padding-right
- padding-before : Section 3.5.101: padding-before
- padding-after : Section 3.5.100: padding-after
- padding-start : Section 3.5.106: padding-start
- padding-end : Section 3.5.103: padding-end
- vertical-align : Section 3.5.140: vertical-align
- space-end : Section 3.5.128: space-end
- space-start : Section 3.5.129: space-start
- writing-mode : Section 3.5.146: writing-mode

3.4.11 fo:inline-sequence

3.4.11.1 Purpose

An inline-sequence is used to group inline flow objects and to assign inherited properties to be shared across them.

3.4.11.2 Description

An inline-sequence formatting object is formatted to produce the series of inline areas produced by each of its children. This object must contain only inline flow objects and holds its content as children.

> **NOTE:** An inline-sequence is useful for specifying inherited properties. For example, a sequence with a specification of a font-style property may be constructed for an italic-emphasis phrase element in a block.

An inline-sequence has no applicable properties.

3.4.11.3 Properties

- id : Section 3.5.68: id

3.4.12 fo:link-end-locator

3.4.12.1 Purpose

Represents a target for link.

3.4.12.2 Description

3.4.12.3 Properties

- href : Section 3.5.61: href
- id : Section 3.5.68: id
- show-content : Section 3.5.124: show-content

3.4.13 fo:list-block

3.4.13.1 Purpose

Creates a block-level area containing a list.

3.4.13.2 Description

The object creates a block-level area containing a list. Its allowed children are either only list-item-label,list-item pairs or only list-item-body objects.

3.4.13.3 Properties

- background-attachment : Section 3.5.4: background-attachment
- background-color : Section 3.5.5: background-color
- background-image : Section 3.5.6: background-image
- background-position : Section 3.5.7: background-position
- background-repeat : Section 3.5.8: background-repeat
- border-color-top : Section 3.5.18: border-color-top
- border-color-bottom : Section 3.5.13: border-color-bottom
- border-color-left : Section 3.5.15: border-color-left
- border-color-right : Section 3.5.16: border-color-right
- border-color-before : Section 3.5.12: border-color-before
- border-color-after : Section 3.5.11: border-color-after

- border-color-start : Section 3.5.17: border-color-start
- border-color-end : Section 3.5.14: border-color-end
- border-width-top : Section 3.5.26: border-width-top
- border-width-bottom : Section 3.5.21: border-width-bottom
- border-width-left : Section 3.5.23: border-width-left
- border-width-right : Section 3.5.24: border-width-right
- border-width-before : Section 3.5.20: border-width-before
- border-width-after : Section 3.5.19: border-width-after
- border-width-start : Section 3.5.25: border-width-start
- border-width-end : Section 3.5.22: border-width-end
- break-before : Section 3.5.28: break-before
- break-after : Section 3.5.27: break-after
- id : Section 3.5.68: id
- end-indent : Section 3.5.34: end-indent
- start-indent : Section 3.5.130: start-indent
- keep : Section 3.5.73: keep
- keep-with-next : Section 3.5.74: keep-with-next
- keep-with-previous : Section 3.5.75: keep-with-previous
- provisional-label-separation : Section 3.5.118: provisional-label-separation
- provisional-distance-between-starts : Section 3.5.117: provisional-distance-between-starts
- space-between-list-rows : Section 3.5.127: space-between-list-rows
- padding-top : Section 3.5.107: padding-top
- padding-bottom : Section 3.5.102: padding-bottom
- padding-left : Section 3.5.104: padding-left
- padding-right : Section 3.5.105: padding-right
- padding-before : Section 3.5.101: padding-before
- padding-after : Section 3.5.100: padding-after
- padding-start : Section 3.5.106: padding-start
- padding-end : Section 3.5.103: padding-end

- space-after : Section 3.5.125: space-after
- space-before : Section 3.5.126: space-before

3.4.14 fo:list-item

3.4.14.1 Purpose

A list-item flow object contains the label and the body of each item; it may be used for overriding and modifying some of the list's properties on a case by case basis.

3.4.14.2 Description

A list-item flow object can only be contained by a list. It is a wrapper for a list-item-label and an list-item-body. It controls their position relative to other items within the list. Most of its properties are typically specified on the list. It controls the position and padding of the label and the body within the list-item and in relation to other list-items in the list.

3.4.14.3 Properties

- background-attachment : Section 3.5.4: background-attachment
- background-color : Section 3.5.5: background-color
- background-image : Section 3.5.6: background-image
- background-position : Section 3.5.7: background-position
- background-repeat : Section 3.5.8: background-repeat
- border-color-top : Section 3.5.18: border-color-top
- border-color-bottom : Section 3.5.13: border-color-bottom
- border-color-left : Section 3.5.15: border-color-left
- border-color-right : Section 3.5.16: border-color-right
- border-color-before : Section 3.5.12: border-color-before
- border-color-after : Section 3.5.11: border-color-after
- border-color-start : Section 3.5.17: border-color-start
- border-color-end : Section 3.5.14: border-color-end
- border-width-top : Section 3.5.26: border-width-top
- border-width-bottom : Section 3.5.21: border-width-bottom
- border-width-left : Section 3.5.23: border-width-left

- border-width-right : Section 3.5.24: border-width-right
- border-width-before : Section 3.5.20: border-width-before
- border-width-after : Section 3.5.19: border-width-after
- border-width-start : Section 3.5.25: border-width-start
- border-width-end : Section 3.5.22: border-width-end
- id : Section 3.5.68: id
- padding-top : Section 3.5.107: padding-top
- padding-bottom : Section 3.5.102: padding-bottom
- padding-left : Section 3.5.104: padding-left
- padding-right : Section 3.5.105: padding-right
- padding-before : Section 3.5.101: padding-before
- padding-after : Section 3.5.100: padding-after
- padding-start : Section 3.5.106: padding-start
- padding-end : Section 3.5.103: padding-end
- space-end : Section 3.5.128: space-end
- space-start : Section 3.5.129: space-start
- space-after : Section 3.5.125: space-after
- space-before : Section 3.5.126: space-before

3.4.15 fo:list-item-body

3.4.15.1 Purpose

The item-body flow object holds the components (usually blocks) for a list item. It controls styling defaults for the body, the spacing between lines and between paras within the list item, break precedences for line and paragraphs within the list item.

3.4.15.2 Description

The item's body contains the content of the item, generally in the form of blocks.

3.4.15.3 Properties

- background-attachment : Section 3.5.4: background-attachment
- background-color : Section 3.5.5: background-color

- background-image : Section 3.5.6: background-image
- background-position : Section 3.5.7: background-position
- background-repeat : Section 3.5.8: background-repeat
- border-color-top : Section 3.5.18: border-color-top
- border-color-bottom : Section 3.5.13: border-color-bottom
- border-color-left : Section 3.5.15: border-color-left
- border-color-right : Section 3.5.16: border-color-right
- border-color-before : Section 3.5.12: border-color-before
- border-color-after : Section 3.5.11: border-color-after
- border-color-start : Section 3.5.17: border-color-start
- border-color-end : Section 3.5.14: border-color-end
- border-width-top : Section 3.5.26: border-width-top
- border-width-bottom : Section 3.5.21: border-width-bottom
- border-width-left : Section 3.5.23: border-width-left
- border-width-right : Section 3.5.24: border-width-right
- border-width-before : Section 3.5.20: border-width-before
- border-width-after : Section 3.5.19: border-width-after
- border-width-start : Section 3.5.25: border-width-start
- border-width-end : Section 3.5.22: border-width-end
- font-family : Section 3.5.43: font-family
- system-font : Section 3.5.135: system-font
- font-size : Section 3.5.44: font-size
- font-size-adjust : Section 3.5.45: font-size-adjust
- font-stretch : Section 3.5.46: font-stretch
- font-style : Section 3.5.47: font-style
- font-variant : Section 3.5.48: font-variant
- font-weight : Section 3.5.49: font-weight
- glyph-alignment-mode : Section 3.5.54: glyph-alignment-mode
- hyphenation-keep : Section 3.5.64: hyphenation-keep

- id : Section 3.5.68: id
- text-indent : Section 3.5.138: text-indent
- end-indent : Section 3.5.34: end-indent
- start-indent : Section 3.5.130: start-indent
- keep : Section 3.5.73: keep
- orphans : Section 3.5.98: orphans
- widows : Section 3.5.141: widows
- keep-with-next : Section 3.5.74: keep-with-next
- keep-with-previous : Section 3.5.75: keep-with-previous
- language : Section 3.5.78: language
- line-height : Section 3.5.84: line-height
- line-height-option : Section 3.5.85: line-height-option
- min-leading : Section 3.5.94: min-leading
- min-post-line-spacing : Section 3.5.95: min-post-line-spacing
- min-pre-line-spacing : Section 3.5.96: min-pre-line-spacing
- line-spacing-precedence : Section 3.5.87: line-spacing-precedence
- padding-top : Section 3.5.107: padding-top
- padding-bottom : Section 3.5.102: padding-bottom
- padding-left : Section 3.5.104: padding-left
- padding-right : Section 3.5.105: padding-right
- padding-before : Section 3.5.101: padding-before
- padding-after : Section 3.5.100: padding-after
- padding-start : Section 3.5.106: padding-start
- padding-end : Section 3.5.103: padding-end
- text-align : Section 3.5.136: text-align
- text-align-last : Section 3.5.137: text-align-last
- text-shadow : Section 3.5.139: text-shadow
- asis-truncate-indicator : Section 3.5.1: asis-truncate-indicator
- asis-wrap-indent : Section 3.5.2: asis-wrap-indent

- asis-wrap-indicator : Section 3.5.3: asis-wrap-indicator
- expand-tabs : Section 3.5.41: expand-tabs
- ignore-record-end : Section 3.5.69: ignore-record-end
- wrap-option : Section 3.5.145: wrap-option
- writing-mode : Section 3.5.146: writing-mode

3.4.16 fo:list-item-label

3.4.16.1 Purpose

A list-item-label is used to either enumerate, identify or adorn the list-item's body.

3.4.16.2 Description

A list-item-label can be contained only in a list-item. It can be used for enumerating the list-item. It can control the positioning of the label and its placement with respect tot he list-item-body. The label has content, and is formatted to become the adornment or enumeration of the list-item.

3.4.16.3 Properties

- background-attachment : Section 3.5.4: background-attachment
- background-color : Section 3.5.5: background-color
- background-image : Section 3.5.6: background-image
- background-position : Section 3.5.7: background-position
- background-repeat : Section 3.5.8: background-repeat
- border-color-top : Section 3.5.18: border-color-top
- border-color-bottom : Section 3.5.13: border-color-bottom
- border-color-left : Section 3.5.15: border-color-left
- border-color-right : Section 3.5.16: border-color-right
- border-color-before : Section 3.5.12: border-color-before
- border-color-after : Section 3.5.11: border-color-after
- border-color-start : Section 3.5.17: border-color-start
- border-color-end : Section 3.5.14: border-color-end
- border-width-top : Section 3.5.26: border-width-top
- border-width-bottom : Section 3.5.21: border-width-bottom

- border-width-left : Section 3.5.23: border-width-left
- border-width-right : Section 3.5.24: border-width-right
- border-width-before : Section 3.5.20: border-width-before
- border-width-after : Section 3.5.19: border-width-after
- border-width-start : Section 3.5.25: border-width-start
- border-width-end : Section 3.5.22: border-width-end
- font-family : Section 3.5.43: font-family
- system-font : Section 3.5.135: system-font
- font-size : Section 3.5.44: font-size
- font-size-adjust : Section 3.5.45: font-size-adjust
- font-stretch : Section 3.5.46: font-stretch
- font-style : Section 3.5.47: font-style
- font-variant : Section 3.5.48: font-variant
- font-weight : Section 3.5.49: font-weight
- glyph-alignment-mode : Section 3.5.54: glyph-alignment-mode
- hyphenation-keep : Section 3.5.64: hyphenation-keep
- id : Section 3.5.68: id
- text-indent : Section 3.5.138: text-indent
- end-indent : Section 3.5.34: end-indent
- start-indent : Section 3.5.130: start-indent
- keep : Section 3.5.73: keep
- orphans : Section 3.5.98: orphans
- widows : Section 3.5.141: widows
- keep-with-next : Section 3.5.74: keep-with-next
- keep-with-previous : Section 3.5.75: keep-with-previous
- language : Section 3.5.78: language
- line-height : Section 3.5.84: line-height
- line-height-option : Section 3.5.85: line-height-option
- min-leading : Section 3.5.94: min-leading

- min-post-line-spacing : Section 3.5.95: min-post-line-spacing
- min-pre-line-spacing : Section 3.5.96: min-pre-line-spacing
- line-spacing-precedence : Section 3.5.87: line-spacing-precedence
- padding-top : Section 3.5.107: padding-top
- padding-bottom : Section 3.5.102: padding-bottom
- padding-left : Section 3.5.104: padding-left
- padding-right : Section 3.5.105: padding-right
- padding-before : Section 3.5.101: padding-before
- padding-after : Section 3.5.100: padding-after
- padding-start : Section 3.5.106: padding-start
- padding-end : Section 3.5.103: padding-end
- text-align : Section 3.5.136: text-align
- text-align-last : Section 3.5.137: text-align-last
- text-shadow : Section 3.5.139: text-shadow
- asis-truncate-indicator : Section 3.5.1: asis-truncate-indicator
- asis-wrap-indent : Section 3.5.2: asis-wrap-indent
- asis-wrap-indicator : Section 3.5.3: asis-wrap-indicator
- expand-tabs : Section 3.5.41: expand-tabs
- ignore-record-end : Section 3.5.69: ignore-record-end
- wrap-option : Section 3.5.145: wrap-option
- writing-mode : Section 3.5.146: writing-mode

3.4.17 fo:page-number

3.4.17.1 Purpose

This object is used to instruct the formatter to construct and present a page-number.

3.4.17.2 Description

This object generates a inline area containing a page number the formatting will generated based on the pagination algorithms it implements.

3.4.17.3 Properties

- id : Section 3.5.68: id

3.4.18 fo:queue

3.4.18.1 Purpose

A queue is used to gather content flow objects to be assigned to (placed into) a given area or set of chained-areas.

3.4.18.2 Description

A queue shall not be allowed within the content of any formatting object except a page-sequence. The queue holds a sequence or tree of formatting-objects that is to be presented in a like-named area of the layout defined by the simple-page-master.

3.4.18.3 Properties

- id : Section 3.5.68: id
- queue-name : Section 3.5.119: queue-name

3.4.19 fo:simple-page-master

3.4.19.1 Purpose

A simple-page-master formatting object defines the layout of a page area. Masters may be repeated in accordance with the page-sequence specification.

3.4.19.2 Description

A simple-page-master is formatted to produce a sequence of page areas.

NOTE: The simple-page-master is intended for systems that wish to provide a very simple page layout facility. Future versions of this specification will support more complex page layouts constructed using the page-master and column-set formatting objects.

A simple-page-master shall be allowed only within the page-sequence.

The simple-page-master supports only the sequential-tiled-page-model, with an ordered set of up to 5 of the following areas: header, body, footer, end-side, and start-side. The user may specify the size (height or width) of the header, footer, end-side, and start-side areas and the separation distances between the adjacent areas. The height of the body area is the page's size (page-height for horizontal writing-modes, and page-width for vertical writing-modes) minus the sum of the header and footer heights, the separations between the areas, and the page's margin in the block-progression-direction.

The stacking direction of the areas, the page and area heights and separation distances are in the direction specified by the writing-mode's block-progression-direction.

The width of each area is the full available distance in the inline-progression-direction after subtracting the page's margin (and may not be negative).

A simple-page-master may use up to 6 associated queues. These queues are not direct children of the page-sequence (but are associated with it by name or via an explicit mapping table):

title

> For online presentations only, this object holds a single title textline to be presented in the window title bar when this simple-page-master is being viewed.

> If provided for print environments, this object is ignored.

> If there is too much text for the title area, the browser may truncate the presentation.

> The content of a title is repeated on each page by replaying the title queue after the body area is processed. (This allows for proper presentation of "dictionary"-style running headers/footers.)

header

> Holds the content to be placed in the header area(s).

> For print and online environments, this object holds a set of information that is presented in a separate area at the top of the page or window.

> If there is too much text for the header area, the presentation may be truncated/clipped.

> The content of a header is repeated on each page by replaying the header queue after the body area is processed. (This allows for proper presentation of "dictionary"-style running headers/footers.)

footer

> Holds the content to be placed in the footer area(s).

> For print and online environments, this holds a set of information that is presented in a separate area at the bottom of the page or window.

If there is too much text for the footer area, the presentation may be truncated/clipped.

The content of a footer is repeated on each page by replaying the footer queue after the body area is processed. (This allows for proper presentation of "dictionary"-style running headers/footers.)

start-side

Holds the content to be placed in the start-side area(s).

For print and online environments, this object holds a set of information that is presented in a separate area at the starting edge (as specified by the page-writing-mode property) of the page or window.

If there is too much text for the start-side area, the presentation may be truncated/clipped.

The content of a start-side area is repeated on each page by replaying the start-side queue after the body area is processed. (This allows for proper presentation of "dictionary"-style running headers/footers.)

end-side

Holds the content to be placed in the end-side area(s).

For print and online environments, this holds a set of information that is presented in a separate area at the ending edge of the page or window.

If there is too much text for the end-side area, the presentation may be truncated/clipped.

The content of a end-side area is repeated on each page by replaying the end-side queue after the body area is processed. (This allows for proper presentation of "dictionary"-style running headers/footers.)

body

Holds the content to be placed in the body area(s).

For print and online environments, this holds the information that is presented in the main area in the middle of the page or window.

In a print environment, if there is too much text for the body area the formatter should create additional pages until all the content is presented.

In a online environment, if there is too much text for the body area the formatter can create additional pages/frames/panels until all the content is presented or it can present the content in a scrolling view.

The simple-page-master defines 5 areas for presentation within the page/window design (formatted area of the page). These are the header, body, footer, start-side, and end-side. It also provides a title, which has no properties defined in the simple-page-master object, but may for example be presented in a browser's title bar.

The following simple-page-masters are the only ones supported in this draft of the standard:

first

The master to be used for the first page in the sequence.

odd

The master to be used for odd-phased pages after the first page in the sequence.

even

The master to be used for even-phased pages after the first page in the sequence.

scrolling

The master to be used for scrolling (non-paged) online presentation.

3.4.19.3 Properties

- background-attachment : Section 3.5.4: background-attachment
- background-color : Section 3.5.5: background-color
- background-image : Section 3.5.6: background-image
- background-position : Section 3.5.7: background-position
- background-repeat : Section 3.5.8: background-repeat
- border-color-top : Section 3.5.18: border-color-top
- border-color-bottom : Section 3.5.13: border-color-bottom
- border-color-left : Section 3.5.15: border-color-left
- border-color-right : Section 3.5.16: border-color-right
- border-color-before : Section 3.5.12: border-color-before
- border-color-after : Section 3.5.11: border-color-after

- border-color-start : Section 3.5.17: border-color-start
- border-color-end : Section 3.5.14: border-color-end
- border-width-top : Section 3.5.26: border-width-top
- border-width-bottom : Section 3.5.21: border-width-bottom
- border-width-left : Section 3.5.23: border-width-left
- border-width-right : Section 3.5.24: border-width-right
- border-width-before : Section 3.5.20: border-width-before
- border-width-after : Section 3.5.19: border-width-after
- border-width-start : Section 3.5.25: border-width-start
- border-width-end : Section 3.5.22: border-width-end
- page-height : Section 3.5.108: page-height
- page-width : Section 3.5.114: page-width
- id : Section 3.5.68: id
- page-margin-left : Section 3.5.110: page-margin-left
- page-margin-right : Section 3.5.111: page-margin-right
- page-margin-bottom : Section 3.5.109: page-margin-bottom
- page-margin-top : Section 3.5.112: page-margin-top
- padding-top : Section 3.5.107: padding-top
- padding-bottom : Section 3.5.102: padding-bottom
- padding-left : Section 3.5.104: padding-left
- padding-right : Section 3.5.105: padding-right
- padding-before : Section 3.5.101: padding-before
- padding-after : Section 3.5.100: padding-after
- padding-start : Section 3.5.106: padding-start
- padding-end : Section 3.5.103: padding-end
- footer-separation : Section 3.5.51: footer-separation
- header-separation : Section 3.5.57: header-separation
- end-side-separation : Section 3.5.36: end-side-separation
- start-side-separation : Section 3.5.132: start-side-separation

- body-overflow : Section 3.5.9: body-overflow
- footer-overflow : Section 3.5.50: footer-overflow
- header-overflow : Section 3.5.56: header-overflow
- end-side-overflow : Section 3.5.35: end-side-overflow
- start-side-overflow : Section 3.5.131: start-side-overflow
- footer-size : Section 3.5.52: footer-size
- header-size : Section 3.5.58: header-size
- end-side-size : Section 3.5.37: end-side-size
- start-side-size : Section 3.5.133: start-side-size
- page-master-name : Section 3.5.113: page-master-name
- page-width : Section 3.5.114: page-width
- body-writing-mode : Section 3.5.10: body-writing-mode
- end-side-writing-mode : Section 3.5.38: end-side-writing-mode
- start-side-writing-mode : Section 3.5.134: start-side-writing-mode
- footer-writing-mode : Section 3.5.53: footer-writing-mode
- header-writing-mode : Section 3.5.59: header-writing-mode
- page-writing-mode : Section 3.5.115: page-writing-mode

3.5 Formatting Properties

3.5.1 asis-truncate-indicator

3.5.1.1 Allowed Values

One of the following:

- none :

A character (See Section 3.6.5: Char).

3.5.1.2 Purpose

Specifies the character (or lack of) to be inserted when truncating content.

3.5.1.3 Description

This property controls what character is inserted with asis content is truncated. If the property value is 'none', no character will be inserted.

3.5.2 asis-wrap-indent

3.5.2.1 Allowed Values

A signed length (See Section 3.6.7: Signed Length).

3.5.2.2 Purpose

Specifies the indentation when asis content is wrapped.

3.5.3 asis-wrap-indicator

3.5.3.1 Allowed Values

One of the following:

*   none :

A character (See Section 3.6.5: Char).

3.5.3.2 Purpose

Specifies the chracter to be used to indicate when asis content is wrapped.

3.5.4 background-attachment

3.5.4.1 Allowed Values

One of the following:

*   fixed :
*   scroll : (Default)

3.5.4.2 Purpose

Specifies if the background image (see 'background-image') should be fixed to the viewport or scroll with the document.

3.5.5 background-color

3.5.5.1 Allowed Values

One of the following:

- transparent : (Default)

A color (See Section 3.6.14: Color).

3.5.5.2 Purpose

Describes the background color of a formatting object.

3.5.6 background-image

3.5.6.1 Allowed Values

One of the followin:

- none : (Default)

A URI (See Section 3.6.20: URI).

3.5.6.2 Purpose

Specifies an image that should be presented in the background.

3.5.7 background-position

3.5.7.1 Allowed Values

One of the following:

- center :
- left :
- right :
- bottom :
- middle :
- top :

A an x-y coordinate (See Section 3.6.6: Coordinate).

3.5.7.2 Purpose

Specifies the background image of a formatting object.

3.5.8 background-repeat

3.5.8.1 Allowed Values

One of the following:

- no-repeat :
- repeat : (Default)
- repeat-x :
- repeat-y :

3.5.8.2 Purpose

Specifies if and how a background image (see 'background-image') should be tiled.

3.5.9 body-overflow

3.5.9.1 Allowed Values

One of the following:

- auto :
- hidden :
- scroll :
- visible :

3.5.9.2 Purpose

Specifies the overflow behavior for the body area. (See overflow).

3.5.9.3 Description

Defines behavior when content is larger than region. (See also XSL:flow-type)

3.5.10 body-writing-mode

3.5.10.1 Allowed Values

One of the following:

- bt-lr :
- bt-rl :

- lr-alternating-rl-bt :
- lr-alternating-rl-tb :
- lr-bt :
- lr-inverting-rl-bt :
- lr-inverting-rl-tb :
- lr-tb :
- rl-bt :
- rl-tb :
- tb-lr :
- tb-rl :
- tb-rl-in-rl-pairs :
- use-page-writing-mode :

3.5.10.2 Purpose

Specifies the writing mode within the body of a simple-page-master.

3.5.10.3 Description

See the writing-mode property.

3.5.11 border-color-after

3.5.11.1 Allowed Values

One of the following:

- transparent :

A color (See Section 3.6.14: Color).

3.5.11.2 Purpose

Specifies the color of the after border.

3.5.12 border-color-before

3.5.12.1 Allowed Values

One of the following:

- transparent :

A color (See Section 3.6.14: Color).

Defaults to black from the transparent color space.

3.5.12.2 Purpose

Specifies the color of the before border.

3.5.13 border-color-bottom

3.5.13.1 Allowed Values

One of the following:

- transparent :

A color (See Section 3.6.14: Color).

Defaults to black from the transparent color space.

3.5.13.2 Purpose

Specifies the color of the bottom border.

3.5.14 border-color-end

3.5.14.1 Allowed Values

One of the following:

- transparent :

A color (See Section 3.6.14: Color).

Defaults to black from the transparent color space.

3.5.14.2 Purpose

Specifies the color of the end border.

3.5.15 border-color-left

3.5.15.1 Allowed Values

One of the following:

- transparent :

A color (See Section 3.6.14: Color).

Defaults to black from the transparent color space.

3.5.15.2 Purpose

Specifies the color of the left border.

3.5.16 border-color-right

3.5.16.1 Allowed Values

One of the following:

- transparent :

A color (See Section 3.6.14: Color).

Defaults to black from the transparent color space.

3.5.16.2 Purpose

Specifies the color of the right border.

3.5.17 border-color-start

3.5.17.1 Allowed Values

One of the following:

- transparent :

A color (See Section 3.6.14: Color).

Defaults to black from the transparent color space.

3.5.17.2 Purpose

Specifies the color of the start border.

3.5.18 border-color-top

3.5.18.1 Allowed Values

One of the following:

* transparent :

A color (See Section 3.6.14: Color).

Defaults to black from the transparent color space.

3.5.18.2 Purpose

Specifies the color of the top border.

3.5.19 border-width-after

3.5.19.1 Allowed Values

An unsigned length (See Section 3.6.8: Unsigned Length).

3.5.19.2 Purpose

Specifies the width of the after border.

3.5.20 border-width-before

3.5.20.1 Allowed Values

An unsigned length (See Section 3.6.8: Unsigned Length).

3.5.20.2 Purpose

Specifies the width of the before border.

3.5.21 border-width-bottom

3.5.21.1 Allowed Values

An unsigned length (See Section 3.6.8: Unsigned Length).

3.5.21.2 Purpose

Specifies the width of the bottom border.

3.5.22 border-width-end

3.5.22.1 Allowed Values

An unsigned length (See Section 3.6.8: Unsigned Length).

3.5.22.2 Purpose

Specifies the width of the end border.

3.5.23 border-width-left

3.5.23.1 Allowed Values

An unsigned length (See Section 3.6.8: Unsigned Length).

3.5.23.2 Purpose

Specifies the width of the left border.

3.5.24 border-width-right

3.5.24.1 Allowed Values

An unsigned length (See Section 3.6.8: Unsigned Length).

3.5.24.2 Purpose

Specifies the width of the right border.

3.5.25 border-width-start

3.5.25.1 Allowed Values

An unsigned length (See Section 3.6.8: Unsigned Length).

3.5.25.2 Purpose

Specifies the width of the start border.

3.5.26 border-width-top

3.5.26.1 Allowed Values

An unsigned length (See Section 3.6.8: Unsigned Length).

3.5.26.2 Purpose

Specifies the width of the top border.

3.5.27 break-after

3.5.27.1 Allowed Values

One of the following:

- auto-page :
- column :
- column-group :
- none : (Default)
- page :
- page-region :

3.5.27.2 Purpose

Specifies page break behavior after a formatting object.

3.5.28 break-before

3.5.28.1 Allowed Values

One of the following:

- auto-page :
- column :
- column-group :
- none : (Default)
- page :
- page-region :

3.5.28.2 Purpose

Specifies the page break behavior before a formatting object.

3.5.29 character

3.5.29.1 Allowed Values

A character (See Section 3.6.5: Char).

3.5.29.2 Purpose

Specifies the Unicode character to be substituted/presented.

3.5.30 color

3.5.30.1 Allowed Values

One of the following:

- transparent :

A color (See Section 3.6.14: Color).

3.5.30.2 Purpose

Describes the foreground color of a formatting object's text content.

3.5.31 contents-alignment

3.5.31.1 Allowed Values

One of the following:

- centered :
- end :
- justify :
- start :

3.5.31.2 Purpose

Specifies the alignment of the child areas within the containing area in the block-progression-direction of the containing area.

3.5.32 contents-rotation

3.5.32.1 Allowed Values

One of the following:

- 0 :
- 90 :
- 180 :
- 270 :

3.5.32.2 Purpose

Specifies the counter-clockwise rotation to be applied to the area contents.

3.5.33 destination

3.5.33.1 Allowed Values

One of the following:

- none :

A URI (See Section 3.6.20: URI).

3.5.33.2 Purpose

Specifies the destination for the link when activated.

3.5.34 end-indent

3.5.34.1 Allowed Values

A signed length (See Section 3.6.7: Signed Length).

3.5.34.2 Purpose

Specifies the indent of the end edge of the area in the direction of the inline-progression-direction.

3.5.35 end-side-overflow

3.5.35.1 Allowed Values

One of the following:

- auto :
- hidden :
- scroll :
- visible :

3.5.35.2 Purpose

Specifies the overflow behavior for the end-side area.

3.5.35.3 Description

Defines behavior when content is larger than region. (See also XSL:flow-type)

3.5.36 end-side-separation

3.5.36.1 Allowed Values

An unsigned length (See Section 3.6.8: Unsigned Length).

3.5.36.2 Purpose

Specifies the distance from the edge of the body area to the adjacent end-side area.

3.5.37 end-side-size

3.5.37.1 Allowed Values

An unsigned length (See Section 3.6.8: Unsigned Length).

3.5.37.2 Purpose

Specifies the width of the end-side area. If the corresponding queue content is absent, this space will still be reserved.

3.5.38 end-side-writing-mode

3.5.38.1 Allowed Values

One of the following:

- bt-lr :
- bt-rl :
- lr-alternating-rl-bt :
- lr-alternating-rl-tb :
- lr-bt :
- lr-inverting-rl-bt :
- lr-inverting-rl-tb :
- lr-tb :
- rl-bt :
- rl-tb :
- tb-lr :
- tb-rl :
- tb-rl-in-rl-pairs :
- use-page-writing-mode :

3.5.38.2 Purpose

Specifies the writing-mode within the end-side area of a simple-page-master.

3.5.38.3 Description

See the writing-mode property.

3.5.39 escapement-space-end

3.5.39.1 Allowed Values

A space specification (See Section 3.6.18: Space Specifier).

Minimum

Maximum

0.0pt

Optimal

0.0pt

3.5.39.2 Purpose

Specifies the space following a glyph-area.

3.5.40 escapement-space-start

3.5.40.1 Allowed Values

A space specification (See Section 3.6.18: Space Specifier).

Minimum

Maximum

0.0pt

Optimal

0.0pt

3.5.40.2 Purpose

Specifies the space preceding a glyph-area.

3.5.41 expand-tabs

3.5.41.1 Allowed Values

A boolean value (See Section 3.6.4: Boolean).

3.5.41.2 Purpose

Specifies whether tabs should be expanded according to tab stops.

3.5.42 first-page-master

3.5.42.1 Allowed Values

A name (See Section 3.6.1: Name).

3.5.42.2 Purpose

Specifies the name of the page master formatting object to use for the first page.

3.5.43 font-family

3.5.43.1 Allowed Values

A font name (See Section 3.6.22: Font Name).

3.5.43.2 Purpose

Specifies a prioritized list of font family names and/or generic family names.

3.5.44 font-size

3.5.44.1 Allowed Values

A signed length (See Section 3.6.7: Signed Length).

3.5.44.2 Purpose

Specifies the size of the font.

3.5.44.3 Description

This property specifies the size of the font. The final size of the font depend on the availability of fonts and the value of 'font-size-adjust'.

3.5.45 font-size-adjust

3.5.45.1 Allowed Values

One of the following:

- none :

An unsigned real value (See Section 3.6.16: Unsigned Real).

3.5.45.2 Purpose

Specifies the ideal ratio between the x-height of a font and the size of the font.

3.5.46 font-stretch

3.5.46.1 Allowed Values

One of the following:

- condensed :
- expanded :
- extra-condensed :
- extra-expanded :
- narrower :
- normal :
- semi-condensed :
- semi-expanded :
- ultra-condensed :
- ultra-expanded :
- wider :

3.5.46.2 Purpose

Selects a face of a certain width within a font family.

3.5.47 font-style

3.5.47.1 Allowed Values

One of the following:

- italic :
- normal :
- oblique :
- reverse-normal :
- reverse-oblique :

3.5.47.2 Purpose

Selects a normal (sometimes referred to as "roman" or "upright"), italic, and oblique face within a font family.

3.5.48 font-variant

3.5.48.1 Allowed Values

One of the following:

- normal :
- small-caps :

3.5.48.2 Purpose

Selects between a normal and small-caps variant of a font face.

3.5.49 font-weight

3.5.49.1 Allowed Values

One of the following:

- 100 :
- 200 :
- 300 :
- 400 :
- 500 :
- 600 :
- 700 :
- 800 :
- 900 :
- bold :
- bolder :
- lighter :
- normal :

3.5.49.2 Purpose

Specifies the weight of the font.

3.5.50 footer-overflow

3.5.50.1 Allowed Values

One of the following:

- auto :
- hidden :
- scroll :
- visible :

3.5.50.2 Purpose

Specifies the overflow behavior for the footer area.

3.5.50.3 Description

Defines behavior when content is larger than region. (See also XSL:flow-type)

3.5.51 footer-separation

3.5.51.1 Allowed Values

An unsigned length (See Section 3.6.8: Unsigned Length).

3.5.51.2 Purpose

Specifies the distance between the bottom of the body area to the top of the footer area.

3.5.52 footer-size

3.5.52.1 Allowed Values

An unsigned length (See Section 3.6.8: Unsigned Length).

3.5.52.2 Purpose

Specifies the height of the footer area.

3.5.52.3 Description

Specifies the height of the footer area. If the corresponding queue content is absent, this space will still be reserved.

3.5.53 footer-writing-mode

3.5.53.1 Allowed Values

One of the following:

- bt-lr :
- bt-rl :
- lr-alternating-rl-bt :
- lr-alternating-rl-tb :
- lr-bt :
- lr-inverting-rl-bt :
- lr-inverting-rl-tb :
- lr-tb :
- rl-bt :
- rl-tb :
- tb-lr :
- tb-rl :
- tb-rl-in-rl-pairs :
- use-page-writing-mode :

3.5.53.2 Purpose

Specifies the writing-mode within the footer area of a simple-page-master.

3.5.53.3 Description

See the writing-mode property.

3.5.54 glyph-alignment-mode

3.5.54.1 Allowed Values

One of the following:

- base :
- bottom :

- center :
- font :
- left :
- math-middle :
- middle :
- right :
- top :

3.5.54.2 Purpose

Used to set the textline's placement-path position relative to the origin of the block-level area.

3.5.55 glyph-id

3.5.55.1 Allowed Values

One of the following:

- use-char-map :

A name (See Section 3.6.1: Name).

3.5.55.2 Purpose

Ed. Note: TODO

3.5.56 header-overflow

3.5.56.1 Allowed Values

One of the following:

- auto :
- hidden :
- scroll :
- visible :

3.5.56.2 Purpose

Specifies the overflow behavior for the header area.

3.5.56.3 Description

Defines behavior when content is larger than region. (See also XSL:flow-type)

3.5.57 header-separation

3.5.57.1 Allowed Values

An unsigned length (See Section 3.6.8: Unsigned Length).

Defaults to 18.0pt.

3.5.57.2 Purpose

Specifies the distance between the top of the body area to the adjacent header area.

3.5.58 header-size

3.5.58.1 Allowed Values

An unsigned length (See Section 3.6.8: Unsigned Length).

3.5.58.2 Purpose

Specifies the height of the header area.

3.5.58.3 Description

Specifies the height of the header area. If the corresponding queue content is absent, this space will still be reserved.

3.5.59 header-writing-mode

3.5.59.1 Allowed Values

One of the following:

- bt-lr :
- bt-rl :
- lr-alternating-rl-bt :
- lr-alternating-rl-tb :
- lr-bt :
- lr-inverting-rl-bt :

- lr-inverting-rl-tb :
- lr-tb :
- rl-bt :
- rl-tb :
- tb-lr :
- tb-rl :
- tb-rl-in-rl-pairs :
- use-page-writing-mode :

3.5.59.2 Purpose

Specifies the writing-mode within the header area of a simple-page-master.

3.5.59.3 Description

See the writing-mode property.

3.5.60 height

3.5.60.1 Allowed Values

One of the following:

- auto :

An unsigned length (See Section 3.6.8: Unsigned Length).

3.5.60.2 Purpose

Specifies the content height of boxes.

3.5.61 href

3.5.61.1 Allowed Values

A URI (See Section 3.6.20: URI).

3.5.61.2 Purpose

Specifies a URI target.

3.5.62 hyphenate

3.5.62.1 Allowed Values

A boolean value (See Section 3.6.4: Boolean).

3.5.62.2 Purpose

Specifies whether hyphenation is allowed.

3.5.63 hyphenation-char

3.5.63.1 Allowed Values

A character (See Section 3.6.5: Char).

3.5.63.2 Purpose

Specifies the character to be inserted on automatic hyphenation.

3.5.64 hyphenation-keep

3.5.64.1 Allowed Values

One of the following:

- column :
- none :
- page :
- spread :

3.5.64.2 Purpose

Specifies the hyphenation constraints.

3.5.64.3 Description

This property specifies the hyphenation constraints when at the end of a facing page pair or column.

3.5.65 hyphenation-ladder-count

3.5.65.1 Allowed Values

One of the following:

- none :

An unsigned integer value (See Section 3.6.11: Unsigned Integer).

3.5.65.2 Purpose

Specifies the limit of number of successive hyphenated lines.

3.5.65.3 Description

This property specifies the limit number of successive hyphenated lines.

3.5.66 hyphenation-push-char-count

3.5.66.1 Allowed Values

An unsigned integer value (See Section 3.6.11: Unsigned Integer).

3.5.66.2 Purpose

Specifies the minimum number of characters that must follow an automatically inserted hyphen.

3.5.67 hyphenation-remain-char-count

3.5.67.1 Allowed Values

An unsigned integer value (See Section 3.6.11: Unsigned Integer).

3.5.67.2 Purpose

Specifies the minimum number of characters the must precede an automatically inserted hyphen.

3.5.68 id

3.5.68.1 Allowed Values

One of the following:

- none :

An id(See Section 3.6.2: ID).

3.5.68.2 Purpose

Specifies a unique identifier for this object within all members of the formatter-object-tree.

3.5.68.3 Description

A unique identifier within all members of the formatter-object tree that allows references to this object.

3.5.69 ignore-record-end

3.5.69.1 Allowed Values

A boolean value (See Section 3.6.4: Boolean).

3.5.69.2 Purpose

Specifies whether a record-end shall be ignored.

3.5.69.3 Description

Specifies whether a record-end shall be ignored. If this property is true, then a character with the char-is-record-end qualifier true shall be ignored.

3.5.70 image

3.5.70.1 Allowed Values

A URI (See Section 3.6.20: URI).

3.5.70.2 Purpose

Specifies the location of the image.

3.5.71 inhibit-line-breaks

3.5.71.1 Allowed Values

A boolean value (See Section 3.6.4: Boolean).

3.5.71.2 Purpose

Specifies whether line breaks are allowed.

3.5.71.3 Description

This property controls the behavior of line breaking within or between areas produced by formatting objects. When this property is true no line breaks are allowed.

3.5.72 input-whitespace-treatment

3.5.72.1 Allowed Values

One of the following:

- preserve :
- collapse :
- ignore :

3.5.72.2 Purpose

Specifies treatment of whitespace from the source document.

3.5.73 keep

3.5.73.1 Allowed Values

One of the following:

- avoid :

  Specifies that the formatter should avoid breaking a page inside the areas generated by object to which this property applies.

- auto :

  Specifies that the formatter should use the system default for determining how to breaking a page inside the areas generated by object to which this property applies.

3.5.73.2 Purpose

Describes a page break behavior inside a formatting object.

3.5.74 keep-with-next

3.5.74.1 Allowed Values

A boolean value (See Section 3.6.4: Boolean).

3.5.74.2 Purpose

Specifies whether the formatting object shall be kept in the same area as the next formatting object.

3.5.75 keep-with-previous

3.5.75.1 Allowed Values

A boolean value (See Section 3.6.4: Boolean).

3.5.75.2 Purpose

Specifies whether the formatting object shall be kept in the same area as the previous formatting object.

3.5.76 kern

3.5.76.1 Allowed Values

A boolean value (See Section 3.6.4: Boolean).

3.5.76.2 Purpose

Specifies whether kerning (placement-adjustment) is allowed.

3.5.77 kern-mode

3.5.77.1 Allowed Values

One of the following:

- loose :
- normal : (Default)
- tight :
- touch :

3.5.77.2 Purpose

Specifies the placement adjustment mode.

3.5.78 language

3.5.78.1 Allowed Values

One of the following:

- none :

  disables hyphenation and forces a simple line-breaking strategy. Used for program text and poetry.

- use-document :

  Specifies one should use the language/country/script specified in the source document's xml:lang specifier.

A language (See Section 3.6.21: Language).

3.5.78.2 Purpose

Specifies the language in which the content is written.

3.5.79 left

3.5.79.1 Allowed Values

A signed length (See Section 3.6.7: Signed Length).

3.5.79.2 Purpose

Specifies how far a box's left content edge is offset to the right of the left edge of the box's containing block.

3.5.80 length

3.5.80.1 Allowed Values

An unsigned length (See Section 3.6.8: Unsigned Length).

3.5.80.2 Purpose

Specifies the the length (width).

3.5.81 letter-spacing

3.5.81.1 Allowed Values

A space specification (See Section 3.6.18: Space Specifier).

Minimum

Maximum

   0.0pt

Optimal

   0.0pt

3.5.81.2 Purpose

Specifies spacing behavior between text characters.

3.5.82 letter-spacing-limit

3.5.82.1 Allowed Values

A limit specification (See Section 3.6.19: Limit Specifier).

Minimum

Maximum

- 0.0pt

3.5.82.2 Purpose

Specifies the minimum and maximum amount of letter spacing that may be applied.

3.5.83 ligature

3.5.83.1 Allowed Values

A boolean value (See Section 3.6.4: Boolean).

3.5.83.2 Purpose

Specifies whether ligatures are allowed.

3.5.84 line-height

3.5.84.1 Allowed Values

An unsigned length (See Section 3.6.8: Unsigned Length).

3.5.84.2 Purpose

Specifies the minimal height of the generated areas.

3.5.84.3 Description

In an block formatting context, this property specifies the minimal height of the generated inline areas. In an inline formatting context, this property specifies the exact height of the generated areas.

3.5.85 line-height-option

3.5.85.1 Allowed Values

One of the following:

- consider-shifts :
- disregard-shifts :

3.5.85.2 Purpose

Specifies whether line spacing should consider superior and inferior text in deriving the line height.

3.5.86 line-offset

3.5.86.1 Allowed Values

An unsigned length (See Section 3.6.8: Unsigned Length).

3.5.86.2 Purpose

Specifies the offset distance from the alignment-line to the line.

3.5.87 line-spacing-precedence

3.5.87.1 Allowed Values

One of the following:
- force :
An unsigned integer value (See Section 3.6.11: Unsigned Integer).

3.5.87.2 Purpose

Specifies a precendence for display-space which is generated as a result of the line spacing calculations.

3.5.88 line-thickness

3.5.88.1 Allowed Values

An unsigned length (See Section 3.6.8: Unsigned Length).

3.5.88.2 Purpose

Specifies the thickness of the line.

3.5.89 margin-end

3.5.89.1 Allowed Values

An unsigned length (See Section 3.6.8: Unsigned Length).

Defaults to 0.0pt.

3.5.89.2 Purpose

Specifies the width of the unprinted area measured inward from the end edge of any area.

3.5.89.3 Description

Specifies the distance from the edge of the resulting area that is last in the block-progression-direction's block-progression-direction to the nearest edge of the text area.

3.5.90 margin-start

3.5.90.1 Allowed Values

An unsigned length (See Section 3.6.8: Unsigned Length).

Defaults to 0.0pt.

3.5.90.2 Purpose

Specifies the width of the unprinted area measured inward from the start edge of any area.

3.5.90.3 Description

Specifies the distance from the edge of the resulting area that is first in the block-progression-direction's block-progression-direction to the nearest edge of the text area.

3.5.91 max-height

3.5.91.1 Allowed Values

An unsigned length (See Section 3.6.8: Unsigned Length).

3.5.91.2 Purpose

Specifies the maximum height of the content area.

3.5.92 max-width

3.5.92.1 Allowed Values

An unsigned length (See Section 3.6.8: Unsigned Length).

3.5.92.2 Purpose

Specifies the maximum width of the content area.

3.5.93 merge-link-end-indicators

3.5.93.1 Allowed Values

A boolean value (See Section 3.6.4: Boolean).

3.5.93.2 Purpose

Specifies whether nested links are shown separately.

3.5.93.3 Description

If this link formatting object occurs within another, and merge-link-end-locators is true, then the effect is the same as if the link-end-locators of the ancestor were also link-end-locators of this link. In other words, the link-end-locators of the ancestor and those of this link are potential destinations when the user selects this link. If merge-link-end-locators is false, then only the link-end-locators associated with this link are potential destinations from this link.

3.5.94 min-leading

3.5.94.1 Allowed Values

One of the following:

• none :

An unsigned length (See Section 3.6.8: Unsigned Length).

3.5.94.2 Purpose

Specifies the minimum addition space that must be guaranteed between two lines.

3.5.94.3 Description

This property specifies the minimum addition space that must be guaranteed between two lines. It is used in the calculation of the size of the maximum-line-rectangle.

3.5.95 min-post-line-spacing

3.5.95.1 Allowed Values

One of the following:

• use-font-metrics :

A signed length (See Section 3.6.7: Signed Length).

3.5.95.2 Purpose

Overrides the default ascender-depth.

3.5.95.3 Description

See ascender-depth.

3.5.96 min-pre-line-spacing

3.5.96.1 Allowed Values

One of the following:

• use-font-metrics :

A signed length (See Section 3.6.7: Signed Length).

3.5.96.2 Purpose

Overrides the default ascender-height.

3.5.96.3 Description

See ascender-height.

3.5.97 orientation

3.5.97.1 Allowed Values

One of the following:

- escapement :
- horizontal :
- line-progression :
- vertical :

3.5.97.2 Purpose

Specifies the orientation of a rule.

3.5.98 orphans

3.5.98.1 Allowed Values

An unsigned integer value (See Section 3.6.11: Unsigned Integer).

3.5.98.2 Purpose

Specifies the minimum number of lines of a paragraph that must be left at the bottom of a page.

3.5.99 overflow

3.5.99.1 Allowed Values

One of the following:

- auto :
- hidden :

- scroll :
- visible :

3.5.99.2 Purpose

Specifies the action to be taken if the content of the area does not fit within the dimensions specified for the area.

3.5.99.3 Description

Defines behavior when content is larger than region.

3.5.100 padding-after

3.5.100.1 Allowed Values

An unsigned length (See Section 3.6.8: Unsigned Length).

3.5.100.2 Purpose

Specifies the width of the after padding area.

3.5.101 padding-before

3.5.101.1 Allowed Values

An unsigned length (See Section 3.6.8: Unsigned Length).

3.5.101.2 Purpose

Specifies the width of the before padding area.

3.5.102 padding-bottom

3.5.102.1 Allowed Values

An unsigned length (See Section 3.6.8: Unsigned Length).

3.5.102.2 Purpose

Specifies the width of the bottom padding area.

3.5.103 padding-end

3.5.103.1 Allowed Values

An unsigned length (See Section 3.6.8: Unsigned Length).

3.5.103.2 Purpose

Specifies the width of the end padding area.

3.5.104 padding-left

3.5.104.1 Allowed Values

An unsigned length (See Section 3.6.8: Unsigned Length).

3.5.104.2 Purpose

Specifies the width of the left padding area.

3.5.105 padding-right

3.5.105.1 Allowed Values

An unsigned length (See Section 3.6.8: Unsigned Length).

3.5.105.2 Purpose

Specifies the width of the right padding area.

3.5.106 padding-start

3.5.106.1 Allowed Values

An unsigned length (See Section 3.6.8: Unsigned Length).

3.5.106.2 Purpose

Specifies the width of the start padding area.

3.5.107 padding-top

3.5.107.1 Allowed Values

An unsigned length (See Section 3.6.8: Unsigned Length).

3.5.107.2 Purpose

Specifies the width of the top padding area.

3.5.108 page-height

3.5.108.1 Allowed Values

One of the following:

* auto :

    Specifies that the formatter will determine the height of the page.

An unsigned length (See Section 3.6.8: Unsigned Length).

3.5.108.2 Purpose

Specifies the total height of the page.

3.5.109 page-margin-bottom

3.5.109.1 Allowed Values

An unsigned length (See Section 3.6.8: Unsigned Length).

3.5.109.2 Purpose

Specifies the width of the unprinted area measured inward from the bottom edge of the page area.

3.5.110 page-margin-left

3.5.110.1 Allowed Values

An unsigned length (See Section 3.6.8: Unsigned Length).

3.5.110.2 Purpose

Specifies the width of the unprinted area measured inward from the left edge of the page area.

3.5.111 page-margin-right

3.5.111.1 Allowed Values

An unsigned length (See Section 3.6.8: Unsigned Length).

3.5.111.2 Purpose

Specifies the width of the unprinted area measured inward from the right edge of the page area.

3.5.112 page-margin-top

3.5.112.1 Allowed Values

An unsigned length (See Section 3.6.8: Unsigned Length).

3.5.112.2 Purpose

Specifies the width of the unprinted area measured inward from the top edge of the page area.

3.5.113 page-master-name

3.5.113.1 Allowed Values

One of the following:

- first :
- repeating :
- even :
- odd :
- scrolling :

A name (See Section 3.6.1: Name).

3.5.113.2 Purpose

Specifies the name of the page master.

3.5.114 page-width

3.5.114.1 Allowed Values

One of the following:

- auto :

An unsigned length (See Section 3.6.8: Unsigned Length).

3.5.114.2 Purpose

Specifies the size and orientation of a page box.

3.5.115 page-writing-mode

3.5.115.1 Allowed Values

One of the following:

- bt-lr :
- bt-rl :
- lr-alternating-rl-bt :
- lr-alternating-rl-tb :
- lr-bt :
- lr-inverting-rl-bt :
- lr-inverting-rl-tb :
- lr-tb :
- rl-bt :
- rl-tb :
- tb-lr :
- tb-rl :
- tb-rl-in-rl-pairs :

3.5.115.2 Purpose

Specifies the writing-mode and layout directions for a page in a simple-page-master.

3.5.115.3 Description

See the writing-mode property.

3.5.116 position-point

3.5.116.1 Allowed Values

A an x-y coordinate (See Section 3.6.6: Coordinate).

3.5.116.2 Purpose

Specifies the position in terms of a coordinate.

3.5.117 provisional-distance-between-starts

3.5.117.1 Allowed Values

An unsigned length (See Section 3.6.8: Unsigned Length).

3.5.117.2 Purpose

Specifies the default distance between the start-edge list-item-label and the start-edge of the list-item-body.

3.5.117.3 Description

Used to calculate: magic-label-end = (container? width - (list-block:provisional-distance-between-starts + list-block:start-indent - list-block:provisional-label-separation));

3.5.118 provisional-label-separation

3.5.118.1 Allowed Values

A space specification (See Section 3.6.18: Space Specifier).

Minimum

Maximum

  0.0pt

Optimal

  0.0pt

3.5.118.2 Purpose

Specifies the default distance between the list-item-label and the list-item-body.

3.5.118.3 Description

Used to calculate: magic-label-end = (container? width - (list-block:provisional-distance-between-starts+list-block:start-indent - list-block:provisional-label-separation));

3.5.119 queue-name

3.5.119.1 Allowed Values

A name (See Section 3.6.1: Name).

3.5.119.2 Purpose

Defines the name of the queue.

3.5.120 repeating-even-page-master

3.5.120.1 Allowed Values

A name (See Section 3.6.1: Name).

3.5.120.2 Purpose

Specifies the name of the page master formatting object to use for the repeating even pages.

3.5.121 repeating-odd-page-master

3.5.121.1 Allowed Values

A name (See Section 3.6.1: Name).

3.5.121.2 Purpose

Specifies the name of the page master formatting object to use for the repeating odd pages.

3.5.122 scale-graphic

3.5.122.1 Allowed Values

One of the following:

- max :
- max-uniform :

An signed real value (See Section 3.6.15: Signed Real).

3.5.122.2 Purpose

Specifies whether a graphic should be automatically or manually scaled.

3.5.123 score-spaces

3.5.123.1 Allowed Values

A boolean value (See Section 3.6.4: Boolean).

3.5.123.2 Purpose

Specifies whether the scoring shall be applied to spaces.

3.5.123.3 Description

A value of true means that scoring will be applied to spaces.

3.5.124 show-content

3.5.124.1 Allowed Values

A boolean value (See Section 3.6.4: Boolean).

3.5.124.2 Purpose

Specifies whether the content of the link should be displayed.

3.5.125 space-after

3.5.125.1 Allowed Values

An unsigned length (See Section 3.6.8: Unsigned Length).

3.5.125.2 Purpose

Specifies the desired space following the after-edge any area.

3.5.126 space-before

3.5.126.1 Allowed Values

An unsigned length (See Section 3.6.8: Unsigned Length).

3.5.126.2 Purpose

Specifies the desired space preceding the before-edge any area.

3.5.127 space-between-list-rows

3.5.127.1 Allowed Values

A space specification (See Section 3.6.18: Space Specifier).

Minimum

Maximum

   0.0pt

Optimal

   0.0pt

3.5.127.2 Purpose

Specifies the nominal space between list items within a list block.

3.5.128 space-end

3.5.128.1 Allowed Values

A space specification (See Section 3.6.18: Space Specifier).

Minimum

Maximum

   0.0pt

Optimal

   0.0pt

3.5.128.2 Purpose

Specifies the desired space on the following the end-edge of any area.

3.5.129 space-start

3.5.129.1 Allowed Values

A space specification (See Section 3.6.18: Space Specifier).

Minimum

Maximum

   0.0pt

Optimal

   0.0pt

3.5.129.2 Purpose

Specifies the desired space preceding the start-edge any area.

3.5.130 start-indent

3.5.130.1 Allowed Values

A signed length (See Section 3.6.7: Signed Length).

3.5.130.2 Purpose

Specifies the indent of the starting edge of the area in the direction of the inline-progression-direction.

3.5.131 start-side-overflow

3.5.131.1 Allowed Values

One of the following:

- auto :
- hidden :
- scroll :
- visible :

3.5.131.2 Purpose

Specifies the overflow behavior for the start-side area.

3.5.131.3 Description

Defines behavior when content is larger than region. (See also XSL:flow-type)

3.5.132 start-side-separation

3.5.132.1 Allowed Values

An unsigned length (See Section 3.6.8: Unsigned Length).

3.5.132.2 Purpose

Specifies the distance from the edge of the body area to the adjacent start-side area.

3.5.133 start-side-size

3.5.133.1 Allowed Values

An unsigned length (See Section 3.6.8: Unsigned Length).

3.5.133.2 Purpose

Specifies the width of the start-side area.

3.5.133.3 Description

Specifies the width of the start-side area. If the corresponding queue content is absent, this space will still be reserved.

3.5.134 start-side-writing-mode

3.5.134.1 Allowed Values

One of the following:

- bt-lr :
- bt-rl :
- lr-alternating-rl-bt :
- lr-alternating-rl-tb :

- lr-bt :
- lr-inverting-rl-bt :
- lr-inverting-rl-tb :
- lr-tb :
- rl-bt :
- rl-tb :
- tb-lr :
- tb-rl :
- tb-rl-in-rl-pairs :
- use-page-writing-mode :

3.5.134.2 Purpose

Specifies the writing-mode within the start-side area of a simple-page-master.

3.5.134.3 Description

See the writing-mode property.

3.5.135 system-font

3.5.135.1 Allowed Values

One of the following:

- caption :
- icon :
- menu :
- message-box :
- small-caption :
- status-bar :

3.5.135.2 Purpose

Specifies the system font to be used.

3.5.136 text-align

3.5.136.1 Allowed Values

One of the following:

- centered :
- end :
- justify :
- page-inside :
- page-outside :
- start :

3.5.136.2 Purpose

Describes how inline content of a block is aligned.

3.5.137 text-align-last

3.5.137.1 Allowed Values

One of the following:

- centered :
- end :
- justify :
- page-inside :
- page-outside :
- relative :
- start :

3.5.137.2 Purpose

Specifies the alignment of the last textline in the block in the line-progression-direction determined by the writing-mode.

3.5.137.3 Description

A value of auto specifies that the value of the text-align property shall be used, except when that value is justify or justify-force, in which case, a value of start shall be used.

A value of spread-inside or spread-outside shall be allowed only if the formatting object has an ancestor of class page-master. A value of page-inside or page-outside shall be allowed only if the formatting object has an ancestor of column-set-master.

3.5.138 text-indent

3.5.138.1 Allowed Values

A signed length (See Section 3.6.7: Signed Length).

3.5.138.2 Purpose

Specifies the indentation of the first line of text in a block.

3.5.139 text-shadow

3.5.139.1 Allowed Values

One of the following:

- none :

   Specifies that no shadow should be used for text.

A color (See Section 3.6.14: Color).

3.5.139.2 Purpose

Specifies the shadow effects that should be applied to the text.

3.5.140 vertical-align

3.5.140.1 Allowed Values

One of the following:

- baseline :
- bottom :
- middle :
- sub :
- super :
- text-bottom :

- text-top :
- top :

A signed length (See Section 3.6.7: Signed Length).

3.5.140.2 Purpose

Describes how a formatting object is positioned inside a line box.

3.5.141 widows

3.5.141.1 Allowed Values

An unsigned integer value (See Section 3.6.11: Unsigned Integer).

3.5.141.2 Purpose

Specifies the minimum number of lines of a paragraph that must be left at the top of a page.

3.5.142 width

3.5.142.1 Allowed Values

One of the following:

- auto :

An unsigned length (See Section 3.6.8: Unsigned Length).

3.5.142.2 Purpose

Specifies the content width of boxes.

3.5.143 word-spacing

3.5.143.1 Allowed Values

One of the following:

- normal :

A space specification (See Section 3.6.18: Space Specifier).

Minimum

Maximum

0.0pt

Optimal

0.0pt

3.5.143.2 Purpose

Specifies spacing behavior between words.

3.5.144 word-spacing-limit

3.5.144.1 Allowed Values

A limit specification (See Section 3.6.19: Limit Specifier).

Minimum

Maximum

0.0pt

3.5.144.2 Purpose

Specifies the minimum and maximum amount of word spacing that may be applied.

3.5.144.3 Description

This value indicates the amount of inter-word space to be added to each the normal space between words. The value may be negative (indicating the amount of space to remove). There may be implementation specific limits on the length specified. The application may also adjust inter-word spacing to justify the line.

3.5.145 wrap-option

3.5.145.1 Allowed Values

One of the following:

- normal :
- no-wrap :
- pre :
- asis-overrun :

- asis-truncate :
- asis-wrap :
- wrap :

3.5.145.2 Purpose

Show whitespace inside the formatting object is to be handled.

3.5.146 writing-mode

3.5.146.1 Allowed Values

One of the following:

- bt-lr :

  Specifies:

    - The inline-progression-direction & escapement-progression-direction are set to bottom-to-top.

    - The block-progression-direction and line-progression-direction are top-to-bottom.

    - The shift-direction is right-to-left.

- bt-rl :

  Specifies:

    - The inline-progression-direction & escapement-progression-direction are set to bottom-to-top.

    - The block-progression-direction and line-progression-direction are right-to-left.

    - The shift-direction is left-to-right.

- lr-alternating-rl-bt :

  Specifies:

    - The first line's inline-progression-direction & escapement-progression-direction are set to left-to-right. The second line's inline-progression-direction &

escapement-progression-direction are right-to-left. This alternating direction pattern continues through the end of the block.

- The block-progression-direction and line-progression-direction are bottom-to-top.

- The shift-direction is top-to-bottom.

- lr-alternating-rl-tb :

Specifies:

- The first line's inline-progression-direction & escapement-progression-direction are set to left-to-right. The second line's inline-progression-direction & escapement-progression-direction are right-to-left. This alternating direction pattern continues through the end of the block.

- The block-progression-direction and line-progression-direction are top-to-bottom.

- The shift-direction is bottom-to-top.

- lr-bt :

Specifies:

- The inline-progression-direction & escapement-progression-direction are set to left-to-right.

- The block-progression-direction and line-progression-direction are bottom-to-top.

- The shift-direction is bottom-to-top.

- lr-inverting-rl-bt :

Specifies:

- The first line's inline-progression-direction & escapement-progression-direction are set to left-to-right. The second line is written upside-down in the opposite direction. This alternating direction pattern continues through the end of the block.

- The block-progression-direction and line-progression-direction are bottom-to-top.

- Lines that are written left-to-right have a shift-direction of bottom-to-top. Lines that are written inverted and right-to-left have a shift-direction of top-to-bottom.

- lr-inverting-rl-tb :

  Specifies:

  - The first line's inline-progression-direction & escapement-progression-direction are set to left-to-right. The second line is written upside-down in the opposite direction. This alternating direction pattern continues through the end of the block.

  - The block-progression-direction and line-progression-direction are top-to-bottom.

  - Lines that are written left-to-right have a shift-direction of bottom-to-top. Lines that are written inverted and right-to-left have a shift-direction of top-to-bottom.

- lr-tb :

  Specifies (European, most western languages) :

  - The inline-progression-direction & escapement-progression-direction are set to left-to-right.

  - The block-progression-direction and line-progression-direction are top-to-bottom.

  - The shift-direction is bottom-to-top.

- rl-bt :

  Specifies:

  - The inline-progression-direction & escapement-progression-direction are set to right-to-left.

  - The block-progression-direction and line-progression-direction are bottom-to-top.

  - The shift-direction is bottom-to-top.

- rl-tb :

Specifies (Arabic/Hebrew):

- The inline-progression-direction & escapement-progression-direction are set to right-to-left.
- The block-progression-direction and line-progression-direction are top-to-bottom.
- The shift-direction is bottom-to-top.

- tb-lr :

Specifies (Mongolian, western signage):

- The inline-progression-direction & escapement-progression-direction are set to top-to-bottom.
- The block-progression-direction and line-progression-direction are left-to-right.
- The shift-direction is left-to-right.

- tb-rl :

Specifies (CJK):

- The inline-progression-direction & escapement-progression-direction are set to top-to-bottom.
- The block-progression-direction and line-progression-direction are right-to-left.
- The shift-direction is left-to-right.

- tb-rl-in-rl-pairs :

Specifies (Korea):

- Two characters are placed beside each other in a right-to-left order. These pairs are stacked into a top-to-bottom row (line). Inlines are treated like a character-pair.
- The inline-progression-direction is set to top-to-bottom.
- The block-progression-direction and line-progression-direction are right-to-left.
- The shift-direction is left-to-right.

- use-page-writing-mode :
  - Uses the inherited writing-mode value from the writing-mode of the page.

3.5.146.2 Purpose

This property sets the text orientation, block-progression-direction, line-progression-direction, inline-progression-direction, and escapement-direction.

3.6 Datatypes

3.6.1 Name

An string of characters conforming to the XML NMTOKEN definition.

3.6.2 ID

A string of characters conforming to the XML NMTOKEN definition that is unique within the stylesheet.

3.6.3 IDREF

A string of characters conforming to the XML NMTOKEN definition that uses a ID property value used within the stylesheet.

3.6.4 Boolean

A boolean value where the allowed values are the strings 'true' and 'false'.

3.6.5 Char

A single unicode character value—whitespace is not allowed.

3.6.6 Coordinate

A pair of signed real values separated by a comma.

Ed. Note: Is the comman appropriate here?

3.6.7 Signed Length

A signed length value where a 'length' is a real number plus a unit qualification. .

3.6.8 Unsigned Length

An unsigned length value including zero where a 'length' is a real number plus a unit qualification. .

3.6.9 Positive Length

A positive length value not including zero where a 'length' is a real number plus a unit qualification. .

3.6.10 Signed Integer

A signed integer value which consists of an optional '+' or '-' character followed by a sequence of digits.

3.6.11 Unsigned Integer

An unsigned integer value including zero which consists of a sequence of digits.

3.6.12 Positive Integer

An unsigned integer value not including zero which consists of a sequence of digits.

3.6.13 Percent

A percentage which is a signed real value (e.g. 45.5 is 455/1000).

3.6.14 Color

A color specification where '#xxxxxx' is an RGB value encoded in hexidecimal or a named color.

> **Ed. Note:** How does other color spaces get encoded?

> **Ed. Note:** What set of "named colors" will we use?

3.6.15 Signed Real

A signed real number which consists of an optional '+' or '-' character followed by a sequence of digits followed by an optional '.' character and sequence of digits.

3.6.16 Unsigned Real

An unsigned real number including zero which consists of a sequence of digits followed by an optional '.' character and sequence of digits.

3.6.17 Positive Real

An unsigned real number not including zero which consists of a sequence of digits followed by an optional '.' character and sequence of digits.

3.6.18 Space Specifier

A semi-colon separated triplit of lengths specifying the minimum, maximum, and optimal space lengths respectively.

3.6.19 Limit Specifier

A semi-colon separated pair of lengths specifying the minimum and maximum lengths.

3.6.20 URI

A sequence of characters conforming to a URI value as specified in the URI specification.

Ed. Note: This should refer to the proper specification.

3.6.21 Language

A string of characters conforming to the `xml:lang` attribute value from XML 1.0

3.6.22 Font Name

A string of characters identifying a font.

Ed. Note: Shouldn't this have a standardized format?

3.6.23 Font List

A list of font names separated by whitespace.

3.6.24 Enumeration

A enumerated list of XML NMTOKEN values.

3.6.25 String

A sequence of characters.

3.7 Defined Terms

NOTE: Coordination between CSS and XSL properties and objects is an ongoing process, with the goal of defining a common underlying formatting model. Therefore, some of the object names and definitions, as well as property names, allowed values, and definitions may change as a result of this effort.

alignment-point

This is a the local origin point of an area. It is the point in the area that is used as the positioning reference for placement within a parent or for aligning multiple areas.

allocation-rectangle

The boundary of the portion of an area which is deemed to take up room when placing the area inside a larger area.

area

A "region" is the specification (in a formatting-object) instructing the formatter on how to create one or more areas. An "area" is the result of formatting.

(See the "Formatting Model" section of this specification for more complete descriptions of all types of areas.)

area-container

Area-containers are the highest level objects in the formatted result. They specify portions of a page or portions of another area-container.

Area containers are always placed objects. (They have an x-y coordinate specifying thier placement or they are attached to a designated edge of a parent area-container.)

Area-containers may set a local coordinate space and always set a local writing-mode (which inherits to all areas contained in the container.

(See the "Formatting Model" section of this specification for more complete descriptions of all types of areas.)

block-area

Area-containers contain a set of block-areas. Block areas are stacked (placed sequentially and adjacent to one another) within the area-container..

Block-areas are always stacked objects. They are stacked within the area-container or within another block-area in the direction specified by the block-progerssion-direction (as derived from the active writing-mode). The initial edge of one block-area is normally placed touching the final-edge of the preceding block-area. However, if space-before/space-after is specified or if the parent object has a spread or a space-out property, then spae may be inserted between the block-areas in the stack.

Block-areas may be nested, however, the start-indent and end-indent of a block is measured from the area-container, not from the parent-block.

Blocks may NOT set a local coordinate space nor set a local writing-mode.

(See the "Formatting Model" section of this specification for more complete descriptions of all types of areas.)

line-area

Line-areas are stacked (placed sequentially and adjacent to one another) inside block-areas. They are always the full width of the block-area (except when adjusted by the text-indent and last-line-indent properties.

Line-areas are always stacked objects. They are stacked within the block-area in the direction specified by the active line-progression-direction (as derived from the active writing-mode). The initial edge of one line-area is normally placed touching the final-edge of the preceding line-area. However, if line-spacing is specified or if the parent object has a spread or a space-out property, then space may be inserted between the line-areas in the stack.

Line-areas are always generated by the formatter (there is no formatting-object that corresponds directly to a line-area.) Line-areas may not be nested.

Line-areas may NOT set a local coordinate space nor set a local writing-mode, however, the direction of inline-progression-direction, escapement=progression-direction, shift-direction, and up-direction may change from line-to-line on an algorithmic basis.

(See the "Formatting Model" section of this specification for more complete descriptions of all types of areas.)

inline-area

Inline-areas are stacked (placed sequentially and adjacent to one another) inside line-areas or inside other inline-areas.

Inline-areas are always stacked objects. They are stacked within the line-area in the direction specified by the active inline-progression-direction (as derived from the active writing-mode). The start edge of one inline-area is normally placed touching the end-edge of the preceding inline-area. However, if line-spacing is specified or if the parent object has a justified or a distributed property, then space may be inserted between the inline-areas in the line.

An inline-area is created for each inline-formatting-object. Additional line areas may be generated when an inline-area must be split for line-breaking or hyphenation and may be split for Unicode bidi support. Inline-areas may be nested.

Inline-areas may NOT set a local coordinate space nor set a local writing-mode, however, the direction of inline-progression-direction and escapement-progression-direction may be changed on an algorithmic basis (for Unicode bidi) or by setting the direction property on the inline-formatting-object.

Note that ruby, wari-chu, and emphasizing-mark specify the creation of multiple inline-areas that are placed within a parent inline-area with a number of specific justapositions. To simplify the formatting-model, these are treated as special cases.

(See the "Formatting Model" section of this specification for more complete descriptions of all types of areas.)

glyph-area

Each character (glyph) generates its own inline area.

Glyph-areas are always stacked (placed sequentially and adjacent to one another) objects. They are stacked within the inline-area in the direction specified by the active escapement-progression-direction (as derived from the active writing-mode). The start edge of one glyph-area is normally placed touching the end-edge of the preceding glyph-area. However, if letter-spacing or kerning is specified, then space may be inserted between the glyph-areas.

A glyph-area is created for each glyph (including space glyphs). Several characters may be merged into a single glyph. (This occurs when a ligature or a composite accented character can be substituted for a multi-character sequence. Glyph-areas are the lowest-level text areas and may not be nested.

(See the "Formatting Model" section of this specification for more complete descriptions of all types of areas.)

ascender-height

The distance from an glyph-area's position point to its nominally greatest extent in the direction opposite the line-progression direction. This is a property of the glyph's font as a whole and not of the individual glyph represented.

border

A solid open rectangle surrounding an area's content rectangle, possibly separated by padding.

conditionality

A boolean property indication if the display-space should be suppressed at the if it appears first or last in an area-container.

content-rectangle

The boundary of the portion of the area in which the content of the area appears, including the allocation-rectangles of smaller areas.

descender-depth

The distance from an glyph-area's position point to its nominally greatest extent in the line-progression direction. This is a property of the glyph's font as a whole and not of the individual glyph represented.

directions and edges

XSL uses absolute-direction-specifiers for page layout and for explicit placement of regions/area-containers.

XSL uses relative-direction-specifiers for all stacked (placed sequentially and adjacent to one another) areas (block-level and inline areas).

It also uses consistent and specific definitions for: start, end, before, after, initial, final, middle, midpoint, center, centered, justify, justified, distribute, distributed, spread, and space-out.

Position and alignment specifiers

It should be noted that areas may have either absolute position and alignment specifiers or they may have relative position and alignment specifiers, but they may not have both.

absolute position and alignment specifiers

These terms are values to properties that specify the position of one object within another or adjacent to another or the relative positioning of 2 aligned objects. This set of values are used only when absolute directions are applicable.

(From CSS, except as noted.)

In the vertical direction

One of the following:

bottom

the bottom-edge of

In positions: the bottom edge of an area.

In alignments: the bottommost edge of an area is aligned with the alignment-point of the referenced object, usually the bottommost edge of the container.

Used only when absolute directions are applicable.

middle

(CSS uses center, which is ambiguous and must be resolved based on the context of usage. XSL uses middle to remove this ambiguity.).

In positions: the position halfway between top and bottom.

In alignments: the middle of an area is aligned with the alignment-point of the referenced object, usually the middle of the container.

Used only when absolute directions are applicable.

top

In positions: the top edge of an area.

In alignments: the topmost edge of an area is aligned with the alignment-point of the referenced object, usually the topmost edge of the container.

Used only when absolute directions are applicable.

In the horizontal direction

One of the following:

center

In positions: the position halfway between left and right.

In alignments: the center of an area is aligned with the alignment-point of the referenced object, usually the center of the container.

Used only when absolute directions are applicable.

(Note present tense.)

distribute

In positions: this term should not be used.

In alignments: the contents of the area are stretched or spaced so that it fills the available left-right width, however, additional space is also inserted at the left-edge and right-edge of the area.

Used only when absolute directions are applicable.

(Note present tense.)

justify

In positions: this term should not be used.

In alignments: the contents of the area are stretched or spaced so that it fills the available left-right width.

Used only when absolute directions are applicable.

(Note present tense.)

left

In positions: the left edge of an area.

In alignments: the leftmost edge of an area is aligned with the alignment-point of the referenced object, usually the leftmost edge of the container.

Used only when absolute directions are applicable.

right

In positions: the right edge of an area.sss

In alignments: the rightmost edge of an area is aligned with the alignment-point of the referenced object, usually the rightmost edge of the container.

Used only when absolute directions are applicable.

relative position and alignment specifiers

These terms are values to properties that specify the position of one object within another or adjacent to another or the relative positioning of 2 aligned objects. This set of values are used only when relative directions are applicable.

In the line-progression-direction and the block-progression-direction

One of the following:

after

In positions: The last-edge of an area in the line-/block-progression-direction, or the space after that edge. (If the writing mode is lr-tb, this would be the bottom edge).

In alignments: The item is placed outside the area adjacent to the last-edge (after-edge) of the area.

Used only when relative directions are applicable.

before

In positions: The first-edge of an area in the line-/block-progression-direction, or the space before that edge. (If the writing mode is lr-tb, this would be the top edge).

In alignments: The item is placed outside the area adjacent to the first-edge (before-edge) of the area.

Used only when relative directions are applicable.

final

In positions: The last position (closest to the after-edge) that an area can be placed within its parent container.

In alignments: The object's alignment-point of the referenced object is aligned with the alignment-point of the referenced object (usually the baseline) of the last item placed within the area.

Used only when relative directions are applicable.

initial

In positions: The first position (closest to the before-edge) that an area can be placed within its parent container.

In alignments: The object's alignment-point of the referenced object is aligned with the alignment-point of the referenced object (usually the baseline) of the first item placed within the area.

Used only when relative directions are applicable.

midpoint

In positions: the position halfway between before-edge and after-edge.

In alignments: the center of an area is aligned with the alignment-point of the referenced object, usually the center of the container.

Used only when relative directions are applicable.

(Note midpoint vs. middle.)

spaced-out

In positions: this term should not be used.

In alignments: the contents of the area are stretched or spaced so that it fills the available initial-final height, however, additional space is also inserted at the initial-edge and final-edge of the area.

Used only when relative directions are applicable.

(Note past tense.)

spread

In positions: this term should not be used.

In alignments: the contents of the area are stretched or spaced so that it fills the available initial-final height.

Used only when relative directions are applicable.

(Note past tense.)

In the escapemant-progression-direction and the inline-progression-direction

One of the following:

centered

In positions: the position halfway between start and end.

In alignments: the centered point of an area is aligned with the alignment-point of the referenced object, usually the centered point of the container.

Used only when relative directions are applicable.

(Note past tense.)

end

In positions: the edge of an area closest to the end edge indicated by the first term of the writing-mode that applies to the area. (If the writing mode is lr-tb, this would be the right edge).

In alignments: the end edge of an area is aligned with the alignment-point of the referenced object, usually the end edge of the container.

Used only when relative directions are applicable.

distributed

In positions: this term should not be used.

In alignments: the contents of the area are stretched or spaced so that it fills the available start-end width, however, additional space is also inserted at the start-edge and end-edge of the area.

Used only when relative directions are applicable.

(Note past tense.)

start

In positions: the edge of an area closest to the start edge indicated by the first term of the writing-mode that applies to the area. (If the writing mode is lr-tb, this would be the left edge).

In alignments: the start edge of an area is aligned with the alignment-point of the referenced object, usually the start edge of the container.

Used only when relative directions are applicable.

justified

In positions: this term should not be used.

In alignments: the contents of the area are stretched or spaced so that it fills the available start-end width.

Used only when relative directions are applicable.

(Note past tense.)

direction

The term "direction" should be qualified as described in the following list. All relative positions and progressions in XSL are specified in terms of one or more of these direction specifiers.

The "writing-mode" property is used to set these values as a set.

For some formatting objects, the "direction" property can override one of these (or the subset of the direction specifiers that would be parallel— for example, it may set both the block-progression-direction and the line-progression-direction or override both the inline-progression-direction and the escapement-progression-direction).

block-progression-direction

The direction of progression of sequential block-level area placements as specified by the last term of the writing-mode. (If the writing-mode is lr-tb, the block-progression-direction is top-to-bottom.)

Always perpendicular to the inline-progression-direction.

column-progression-direction

The direction of progression of sequential column area placements as specified by the first term of the writing-mode. (If the writing-mode is lr-tb, the column-progression-direction is left-to-right.)

For writing modes that have alternating or inverting first terms, this direction does not reverse.

escapement-progression-direction

The direction of progression of sequential glyph area placements along the placement-path as specified by the character/glyph information. May be overridden by the direction property. May be the same as or the reverse of the inline-progression-direction. (If the writing-mode is lr-tb, the escapement-progression-direction is left-to-right.)

If unspecified, use the inline-progression-direction specified by the first term of the writing-mode.

For writing modes that have alternating or inverting first terms, this direction reverses accordingly.

inline-progression-direction

The direction of progression of sequential inline areas as specified by the first term of the writing-mode. (If the writing-mode is lr-tb, the inline-progression-direction is left-to-right.)

Usually the same direction as the escapement direction.

Perpendicular to the block-progression direction and the line-progression direction.

For writing modes that have alternating or inverting first terms, this direction reverses accordingly.

line-progression-direction

Perpendicular to the inline-progression-direction, the direction of successive textline placements as specified by the last term of the writing-mode. (If the writing-mode is lr-tb, the line-progression-direction is top-to-bottom.)

Usually the same as the block-progression-direction.

row-progression-direction

The direction of progression of sequential row area placements as specified by the last term of the writing-mode. (If the writing-mode is lr-tb, the row-progression-direction is top-to-bottom.)

shift-direction

The direction of positive shift when characters, inline areas, or scores are shifted perpendicular to the placement-path. Usually the reverse of the line-progression-direction. (If the writing-mode is lr-tb, the shift-direction is bottom-to-top.)

For writing modes that have inverting first terms, this direction reverses accordingly.

up-direction

The direction of the characterÕs up-vector.

For mixed-width-non-joining text, this is usually the same as the shift-direction.

For vertically-written ideographic text, the up-vector is the reverse of the first-term of the writing-mode. (If the writing mode is tb-lr, the up-vector is bottom-to-top.)

For roman text in vertically-written ideographic text, the up-vector is specified by the vertical-roman-orientation property. (If the writing-mode is tb-lr: and vertical-roman-orientation=vertical then the up-direction for roman text is bottom-to-top, however, if the vertical-roman-orientation=perpendicular then the up-direction for roman-text is right-to-left.)

edge

The term "edge" specifies each of the sides of any area, based on writing-mode. "Edge" should be qualified as follows:

after-edge

The area following the current area in the direction specified by the last term of the writing mode. (Also the edge of the current area toward the area following the current area in the direction specified by the last term of the writing mode.)

final-edge

The edge of the current area toward the area following the current area in the direction specified by the last term of the writing mode.

before-edge

The area prior to the current area in the direction specified by the last term of the writing mode. (Also the edge of the current area toward the area prior to the current area in the direction specified by the last term of the writing mode.)

initial-edge

The edge of the current area toward the area prior to the current area in the direction specified by the last term of the writing mode.

end-edge

The area following the current area in the direction specified by the first term of the writing mode. (Also the edge of the current area toward the area following the current area in the direction specified by the first term of the writing mode.)

For writing modes that have alternating or inverting first terms, this direction reverses accordingly.

start-edge

The area prior to the current area in the direction specified by the first term of the writing mode. (Also the edge of the current area toward the area prior to the current area in the direction specified by the first term of the writing mode.)

For writing modes that have alternating or inverting first terms, this direction reverses accordingly.

escapement-point

A designated point of an inline-area which, when the area is placed, is used in determining the containing line-area's new placement-point. It is always on the edge opposite the position-point.

escapement-vector

The vector from the placement-point of an inline-area to its escapement-point.

line

Since we have many kinds of lines, the term will be qualified as follows:

graphic-line

A graphic representation of a line-segment. Used for rules and scores (underscore, overscore, and strike-through).

textline

A sequence of characters (and spaces) arranged along or relative to a common baseline.

margin

We have not resolved all differences between CSS's use of the term margin and XSL's use of the terms display-space or inline-space. The term margin is used for page-margins and cell-margins. It is left as a placeholder in a number of other locations until all the details of the difference between the 2 models can be full resolved.

maximum-line-rectangle

The rectangle associated with a line area which is as wide as the content rectangle in the inline-progression direction, and which in the perpendicular direction stretches from the maximum ascender-height to the maximum descender-depth for the actual fonts and inline-areas placed on the line, as raised and lowered by vertical-align and other adjustments perpendicular to the inline-progression-direction. Used for placing the line when minimum-leading is in effect.

nominal-font

The default font associated with an area. This consists of a fully qualified nominal-font name and font size.

nominal-glyph-height

The height from the descender-depth to the ascender-height of the default font associated with this line-area or inline-area area.

nominal-requested-line-rectangle

The rectangle associated with a line area which is as wide as the content rectangle in the inline-progression direction, and which in the perpendicular direction stretches from the ascender-height to the descender-depth of the nominal-font. Used for placing the line when minimum-leading is in effect.

offset

A fixed height/width adjustment that occurs between 2 objects within an area.

In the absence of futher qualification in the property definition, if this adjustment is positive, the offset object will be displaced in the shift-direction by the distance specified.

Similarly, if this adjustment is negative, the offset object will be displaced in the reverse of shift-direction by the distance specified.

(See also: "space" and "separation".)

padding

The open space between an area's content rectangle and its border.

page-model

Page designs can follow several models:

sequential-tiled-page-model

This is your typical word processor page.

The subareas do not overlap. They are full width and are separated from the preceding subarea by a separation distance measured from the preceding area in the block-progression-direction specified by the writing-mode of the page.

interlocking-tiled-page-model

This is your typical newspaper page.

The subareas do not overlap. Pages consist of rectangular, T, inverted-L shaped areas. They are non-overlapping and touch the adjacent areas (or page margins) on all sides.

simple-freeform-page-model

The origins of the subareas are specified as X-Y coordinates measured from the page origin. Each area then specifies its shape relative to that origin. If areas overlap, they are overlapped in the order that the areas are specified (or in accordance with a z-order property), hiding the information of the underlying area.

exclusionary-freeform-page-model

The origins of the subareas are specified as X-Y coordinates measured from the page origin. Each area then specifies its shape relative to that origin. If areas overlap, they are overlapped in the order that the areas are specified (or in accordance with a z-order property), reshaping the underlying area to wrap around the current area.

placement-path

A progression of items placed adjacently in the inline-progression-direction for inline areas or the block-progression-direction for block-level areas.

placement-point

During the filling of a line-area, the point at which the next inline-area will be placed.

position-point

A designated point on one edge of an inline-area, which is used to align inline-areas along a common placement-path.

precedence

An indication of the importance of one value over another. Display-space and inline-space values with greater precedence take effect over those with lower precedence.

property

An attribute of a formatting-object.

region

The specification, in a formatting object, directing/controlling the creation of an area. (Specifically an area-container.)

qualifier

An attribute of a character. Usually derived through system-dependent font metric and classification services.

queue

(This was "port" in the DSSSL specification.)

separation

> A fixed height/width adjustment that occurs between 2 areas.
>
> If this adjustment is positive, the 2 areas will be separated by the resultant distance.
>
> If this adjustment is negative, the 2 areas will overlap by the resultant distance.
>
> (See also: "space" and "offset".)

space

> A variable height/width adjustment that occurs between 2 areas.
>
> If this adjustment is positive, the 2 areas will be separated by the resultant distance.
>
> If this adjustment is negative, the 2 areas will overlap by the resultant distance.
>
> (See also: "separation" and "offset".)

conditional-space

> A display-space or inline-space with conditionality = true.

display-space

> Space used between line areas or block areas.inline-space
>
> Space used between areas within a line area.

space-character

> The character at codepoint 0x20 (ascii-space).

space-resolution-rules

> The rules used to resolve how several adjacent display spaces or inline spaces are combined into a single display space or inline space.

Appendix A

DTD for XSL Stylesheets

The following entity can be used to construct a DTD for XSL stylesheets that create instances of a particular result DTD. Before referencing the entity, the stylesheet DTD must define a result-elements parameter entity listing the allowed result element types. For example:

```
<!ENTITY % result-elements "
    | fo:inline-sequence
    | fo:block
">

<!ENTITY % instructions "
    | xsl:apply-templates
    | xsl:apply-imports
    | xsl:for-each
    | xsl:value-of
    | xsl:number
    | xsl:counter
    | xsl:counters
    | xsl:counter-increment
    | xsl:counter-reset
    | xsl:counter-scope
    | xsl:choose
    | xsl:if
    | xsl:contents
    | xsl:invoke
    | xsl:text
    | xsl:pi
    | xsl:comment
    | xsl:element
    | xsl:attribute
```

```
    | xsl:use
    | xsl:copy
">

<!ENTITY % template "
 (#PCDATA
  %instructions;
  %result-elements;)*
">

<!ENTITY % space-att "xml:space (default|preserve) #IMPLIED">
 <!ELEMENT xsl:stylesheet
 (xsl:import*,
  (xsl:include
  | xsl:id
  | xsl:strip-space
  | xsl:preserve-space
  | xsl:macro
  | xsl:attribute-set
  | xsl:constant
  | xsl:template)*)
 >

<!ATTLIST xsl:stylesheet
   result-ns NMTOKEN #IMPLIED
   default-space (preserve|strip) "preserve"
   indent-result (yes|no) "no"
   id ID #IMPLIED
   xmlns:xsl CDATA #FIXED "http://www.w3.org/TR/WD-xsl"
   %space-att;
 >

<!-- Used for attribute values that are URIs.-->
<!ENTITY % URI "CDATA">

<!-- Used for attribute values that are patterns.-->
<!ENTITY % pattern "CDATA">
```

```
<!— Used for attribute values that are a priority. —>
<!ENTITY % priority "NMTOKEN">

<!ELEMENT xsl:import EMPTY>
<!ATTLIST xsl:import href %URI; #REQUIRED>

<!ELEMENT xsl:include EMPTY>
<!ATTLIST xsl:include href %URI; #REQUIRED>

<!ELEMENT xsl:id EMPTY>
<!ATTLIST xsl:id

  attribute NMTOKEN #REQUIRED
  element NMTOKEN #IMPLIED
>

<!ELEMENT xsl:strip-space EMPTY>
<!ATTLIST xsl:strip-space element NMTOKEN #REQUIRED>

<!ELEMENT xsl:preserve-space EMPTY>
<!ATTLIST xsl:preserve-space element NMTOKEN #REQUIRED>

<!ELEMENT xsl:template %template;>
<!ATTLIST xsl:template

  match %pattern; #REQUIRED
  priority %priority; #IMPLIED
  mode NMTOKEN #IMPLIED
  %space-att;
>

<!ELEMENT xsl:value-of EMPTY>
<!ATTLIST xsl:value-of select CDATA #IMPLIED>

<!ENTITY % conversion-atts '
   format CDATA "1"
   xml:lang NMTOKEN #IMPLIED
   letter-value (alphabetic|other) #IMPLIED
   digit-group-sep CDATA #IMPLIED
```

```
        n-digits-per-group NMTOKEN #IMPLIED
        sequence-src %URI; #IMPLIED
  '>

<!ELEMENT xsl:number EMPTY>
<!ATTLIST xsl:number
     level (single|multi|any) "single"
     count CDATA #IMPLIED
     from CDATA #IMPLIED
     %conversion-atts;
  >

<!ELEMENT xsl:counter EMPTY>
<!ATTLIST xsl:counter
   name NMTOKEN #REQUIRED
   %conversion-atts;
  >

<!ELEMENT xsl:counters EMPTY>
<!ATTLIST xsl:counters
   name NMTOKEN #REQUIRED
   %conversion-atts;
  >

<!ELEMENT xsl:counter-increment EMPTY>
<!ATTLIST xsl:counter-increment
   name NMTOKEN #REQUIRED
   amount NMTOKEN #IMPLIED
  >

<!ELEMENT xsl:counter-reset EMPTY>

<!ATTLIST xsl:counter-reset

     name NMTOKEN #REQUIRED
     value NMTOKEN #IMPLIED
  >
```

```
<!ELEMENT xsl:counter-scope %template;>
<!ATTLIST xsl:counter-scope %space-att;>

<!ELEMENT xsl:apply-templates (xsl:sort*)>
<!ATTLIST xsl:apply-templates
   select %pattern; #IMPLIED
   mode NMTOKEN #IMPLIED
>

<!ELEMENT xsl:apply-imports EMPTY>

<!— xsl:sort cannot occur after any other elements or
any non-whitespace character —>

<!ELEMENT xsl:for-each
 (#PCDATA
  %instructions;
  %result-elements;
  | xsl:sort)*
>

<!ATTLIST xsl:for-each
   select %pattern; #REQUIRED
   %space-att;
>

<!ELEMENT xsl:sort EMPTY>
<!ATTLIST xsl:sort
   select %pattern; "."
   lang CDATA #IMPLIED
   data-type (text|number) "text"
   order (ascending|descending) "ascending"
   case-order (upper-first|lower-first) #IMPLIED
>

<!ELEMENT xsl:if %template;>
<!ATTLIST xsl:if
   test %pattern; #REQUIRED
   %space-att;
```

```
>
<!ELEMENT xsl:choose (xsl:when+, xsl:otherwise?)>
<!ATTLIST xsl:choose %space-att;>

<!ELEMENT xsl:when %template;>
<!ATTLIST xsl:when
  test %pattern; #REQUIRED
  %space-att;
>

<!ELEMENT xsl:otherwise %template;>
<!ATTLIST xsl:otherwise %space-att;>

<!ELEMENT xsl:attribute-set (xsl:attribute|xsl:use)*>
<!ATTLIST xsl:attribute-set
  name NMTOKEN #REQUIRED
>

<!ELEMENT xsl:constant EMPTY>
<!ATTLIST xsl:constant
  name NMTOKEN #REQUIRED
  value CDATA #REQUIRED
>

<!- xsl:macro-arg cannot occur after any other elements or
any non-whitespace character ->

<!ELEMENT xsl:macro
  (#PCDATA
  %instructions;
  %result-elements;
  | xsl:macro-arg)*
>

<!ATTLIST xsl:macro
  name NMTOKEN #REQUIRED
  %space-att;
>
```

```
<!ELEMENT xsl:macro-arg EMPTY>
<!ATTLIST xsl:macro-arg
  name NMTOKEN #REQUIRED
  default CDATA #IMPLIED
>

<!- This is allowed only within xsl:macro ->
<!ELEMENT xsl:contents EMPTY>

<!- xsl:arg cannot occur after any other elements or
any non-whitespace character ->

<!ELEMENT xsl:invoke
 (#PCDATA
  %instructions;
  %result-elements;
  | xsl:arg)*
>

<!ATTLIST xsl:invoke
  macro NMTOKEN #REQUIRED
  %space-att;
>

<!ELEMENT xsl:arg EMPTY>
<!ATTLIST xsl:arg
  name NMTOKEN #REQUIRED
  value CDATA #REQUIRED
>

<!ELEMENT xsl:text (#PCDATA)>
<!ATTLIST xsl:text %space-att;>

<!ELEMENT xsl:pi %template;>
<!ATTLIST xsl:pi
  name CDATA #REQUIRED
  %space-att;
>
```

```
<!ELEMENT xsl:element %template;>
<!ATTLIST xsl:element
  name CDATA #REQUIRED
  %space-att;
>

<!ELEMENT xsl:attribute %template;>
<!ATTLIST xsl:attribute
  name CDATA #REQUIRED
  %space-att;
>

<!ELEMENT xsl:use EMPTY>
<!ATTRIBUTE xsl:use attribute-set NMTOKEN #REQUIRED>

<!ELEMENT xsl:comment %template;>
<!ATTLIST xsl:comment %space-att;>

<!ELEMENT xsl:copy %template;>
<!ATTLIST xsl:copy %space-att;>
```

Appendix B

References

B.1 Normative References

W3C XML

World Wide Web Consortium. *Extensible Markup Language (XML) 1.0*. W3C Recommendation. See http://www.w3.org/TR/1998/REC-xml-19980210

W3C XML Names

World Wide Web Consortium. *Namespaces in XML*. W3C Working Draft. See http://www.w3.org/TR/WD-xml-names

B.2 Other References

CSS2

World Wide Web Consortium. *Cascading Style Sheets, level 2 (CSS2)*. W3C Recommendation. See http://www.w3.org/TR/1998/REC-CSS2-19980512

DSSSL

International Organization for Standardization, International Electrotechnical Commission. *ISO/IEC 10179:1996. Document Style Semantics and Specification Language (DSSSL)*. International Standard.

UNICODE TR10

Unicode Consortium. *Draft Unicode Technical Report #10. Unicode Collation Algorithm*. Draft Unicode Technical Report. See http://www.unicode.org/unicode/reports/tr10/index.html.

W3C XML Stylesheet

World Wide Web Consortium. *Associating stylesheets with XML documents.* W3C Working Draft.

See http://www.w3.org/TR/WD-xml-stylesheet

Examples (Non-Normative)

The following is a simple but complete stylesheet.

```
<?xml version='1.0'?>
<xsl:stylesheet xmlns:xsl="http://www.w3.org/TR/WD-xsl"
                xmlns:fo="http://www.w3.org/TR/WD-xsl/FO"
                result-ns="fo"
                indent-result="yes">
<xsl:template match='/'>
 <fo:basic-page-sequence font-family="serif">
  <fo:simple-page-master page-master-name='scrolling'/>
  <fo:queue queue-name='body'>
   <xsl:apply-templates/>
  </fo:queue>
 </fo:basic-page-sequence>
</xsl:template>

<xsl:template match="title">
 <fo:block font-weight="bold">
  <xsl:apply-templates/>
 </fo:block>
</xsl:template>

<xsl:template match="p">
 <fo:block>
  <xsl:apply-templates/>
 </fo:block>
</xsl:template>
```

```
<xsl:template match="emph">
 <fo:inline-sequence font-style="italic">
  <xsl:apply-templates/>
 </fo:inline-sequence>
</xsl:template>
</xsl:stylesheet>
```

With the following source document

```
<doc>
<title>An example</title>
<p>This is a test.</p>
<p>This is <emph>another</emph> test.</p>
</doc>
```

it would produce the following result

```
<fo:basic-page-sequence xmlns:fo="http://www.w3.org/TR/WD-xsl/FO"
   font-family="serif">
<fo:simple-page-master page-master-name="scrolling"/>
<fo:queue queue-name="body">
<fo:block font-weight="bold">An example</fo:block>
<fo:block>This is a test.</fo:block>
<fo:block>This is <fo:inline-sequence
   font-style="italic">another</fo:inline-sequence> test.</fo:block>
</fo:queue>
</fo:basic-page-sequence>
```

Design Principles (Non-Normative)

In the design of any language, trade-offs in the solution space are necessary. To aid in making these trade-offs the follow design principles were used:

XSL should support browsing, printing, and interactive editing and design tools

XSL should be capable of specifying presentations for traditional and Web environments

XSL should support interaction with structured information, as well as presentation of it.

XSL should support all kinds of structured information, including both data and documents.

XSL should support both visual and non-visual presentations.

XSL should be a declarative language.

XSL should be optimized to provide simple specifications for common formatting tasks and not preclude more sophisticated formatting tasks.

XSL should provide an extensibility mechanism

The number of optional features in XSL should be kept to a minimum.

XSL should provide the formatting functionality of at least DSSSL and CSS

XSL should leverage other recommendations and standards.

XSL should be expressed in XML syntax.

XSL stylesheets should be human-readable and reasonably clear.

Terseness in XSL markup is of minimal importance.

Appendix E

Acknowledgements (Non-Normative)

The following have contributed to authoring this draft:

Sharon Adler, Inso Corporation

Anders Berglund, Inso Corporation

Jeff Caruso, Bitstream (Formatting Model, Defined Terms)

Paul Grosso, ArborText

Eduardo Gutentag, Sun Microsystems

Chris Lilley, W3C

Chris Maden, O'Reilly & Associates

Jonathan Marsh, Microsoft Corporation

Alex Milowski, Veo Systems (formatting objects and properties database)

Henry S. Thompson, University of Edinburgh

Paul Trevithick, Bitstream

Norman Walsh, ArborText

Steve Zilles, Adobe

Changes from Previous Public Working Draft (Non-Normative)

The following is a summary of changes in the Tree Construction part since the previous public working draft.

`xsl:process` and `xsl:process-children` have been combined into `xsl:apply-templates`.

The expr attribute of `xsl:value-of` has been renamed to select.

Support for comments has been added.

Support for processing instructions has been added.

Support for text nodes has been added.

Support for result tree numbering has been added.

Support for sorting has been added.

The xsl:copy element has been added.

The xsl:element element has been added.

The xsl:attribute element has been added.

Attribute patterns have been changed: the syntax is `@foo` rather than attribute(foo); they can be used as match patterns and select patterns; `@*` can be used to match all attributes.

The argument to `id()` must now be quoted. Select patterns can also be used as an argument.

The syntax for patterns has been reworked; it is now more general than before.

The syntax for quoting namespaces has been changed.

Specificity has been removed.

Priorities can be real numbers.

Support for processing modes has been added.

`xsl:apply-imports` has been added.

`define`—has been removed from the name of `top-level` elements. `xsl:attribute-set` now contains `xsl:attribute` elements.

The `xsl:use` attribute has been replaced by an `xsl:use` element.

The default namespace (as declared with the xmlns attribute) is not used for element type names in patterns.

The `ancestor-or-self` function has been added.

About toExcel's Open Documents Standards Library

Welcome to the world of Open Publishing™ with toExcel.

The book you hold in your hand is just one part of toExcel's revolutionary publishing initiative, bringing important online and other documents to the public in printed form…quickly and efficiently.

toExcel is actively working with Web sites and other information providers to distribute information to the widest possible audience via our unique on-demand publishing technology. We are committed to bringing into print the titles the public needs and wants…from the works of the World Wide Web Consortium to the latest information from the open source movement. We get new and updated titles into your hands fast. What's more, all toExcel books in the Open Document Standards Library are always available to be read online, free at our site, in keeping with the core philosophy of the open documents movement.

Each title in toExcel Open Documents series is a printed version of the latest industry-accepted specifications and contains the complete, unedited text of the original document. toExcel provides this book as a service to the developers' community for use as a handy desktop companion, saving you the time and expense of printing the documentation.

You can learn more about toExcel and how you can be a part of the on-demand publishing revolution by visiting our Web site at www.toExcel.com. You can also give us your feedback and let us know what online materials you'd like us to publish by e-mailing feedback@toExcel.com. We value your opinion.

Kenzi Sugihara
Publisher

About the W3C

The W3C was founded in October 1994 to develop common standards and protocols for the World Wide Web. The W3C is an international industry consortium, jointly hosted by the Massachusetts Institute of Technology Laboratory for Computer Science [MIT/LCS] in the United States; the Institut National de Recherché en Informatique et en Automatique [INRIA] in Europe; and the Keio University Shonan Fujisawa Campus in Japan. Services provided by the Consortium include: a repository of information about the World Wide Web for developers and users; reference code implementations to embody and promote standards; and various prototype and sample applications to demonstrate use of new technology.

For more information about the W3C see http://www.w3c.org/

More Titles in the toExcel Open Docs Series

Cascading Style Sheets Specification, Level 1

available 6/99
ISBN 1-158348-252-0

Ideal for program designers, HTML Web page authors, and others who need to keep abreast of current publishing standards for the World Wide Web, this book describes how to attach a style sheet to an HTML document so that its appearance (fonts, colors, spacing) can be accurately defined and explains the "cascading" nature of style sheets.

Cascading Style Sheets Specification, Level 2

available 6/99
ISBN 1-53848-253-9

A companion to CSS Level 1, this second book contains the complete and most up-to-date version currently available of the CSS2 specification, an enhancement of the earlier CSS1 specifications, that provide greater control and flexibility in rendering a page on screen or paper.

Extensible Markup Language (XML) 1.0 Specifications

available 6/99
ISBN 1-58348-256-3

Representing the future of the World Wide Web, the Exensible Markup Language (XML) provides for an almost limitless variety of text and formatting for Web pages and other electronic documentation. The XML 1.0 specifications are the industry standard recommendation for this important new technology.

toExcel Orders
Phone: 877-823-9235 (877-82EXCEL)
Fax: 408-260-3067
http://www.toExcel.com

Document Object Model Specification, Level 1

available 6/99
ISBN 1-58348-254-7

A handy resource for HTML Web page authors, Web and Internet program developers, Java and JavaScript programmers, and anyone else who publishes documents on the World Wide Web, this book describes what the Document Object Model is, and how it's used and includes full descriptions of all definitions used in the DOM Level 1 specification.

Document Object Model Specification, Level 2

available 6/99
ISBN 1-58348-255-5

The goal of the DOM specification is to define a programmatic interface for XML and HTML. Document Object Model Level 2 builds on DOM Level 1 by adding interfaces for a Cascading Style Sheets object model, an event model, and a query interface, among others. Specification 2 is designed to be a handy desktop companion, saving you the time and expense of printing the documentation yourself and for use when you can't be online.

toExcel Orders
Phone: 877-823-9235 (877-82EXCEL)
Fax: 408-260-3067
http://www.toExcel.com

HTML 3.2 Reference Specification

available 6/99
ISBN 1-58348-258-X

This book is the complete text of the latest available version of the HTML 3.2 specifications and reference manual (also includes the HTML 2.0 specifications). It is a must-have resource for HTML Web page authors, Internet program developers, information technology managers, and anyone else who publishes documents on the World Wide Web.

HTML 4.0 Reference Specification

available 6/99
ISBN 1-58348-259-8

HTML is the most common method to distribute documents on the World Wide Web and gives authors the means to publish online documents with headings, text, tables, lists, photos, and more. This book contains the complete text of the latest available version of the HTML 4.0 specifications and reference manual, as published by the World Wide Web Consortium (W3C), an independent and international standards body devoted to furthering Web and Internet technologies.

toExcel Orders
Phone: 877-823-9235 (877-82EXCEL)
Fax: 408-260-3067
http://www.toExcel.com

Communicate with toExcel Online

There's lots to do at www.toExcel.com including:

Read Entire Books Online...Free

At toExcel, you the opportunity to read this entire book and hundreds more online. You get to try it before you buy it. Our readers get more than just a description, table of contents and reviews. They can make their decision to buy based on viewing the whole book online at toExcel's ReaderCentral.

Get Hard-To-Find Titles

toExcel is amassing a huge collection of out-of-print titles and republishing them. If you're an Apple fan, you can get *Danny Goodman's AppleScript*™ *Handbook*, in a brand new printing, from toExcel.

Have Your Say

We value your opinion. At toExcel you can comment on each and every book and participate in discussions with other readers and authors. You can also e-mail confidential feedback to us at feedback@toExcel.com.

Decide What We Should Publish

toExcel is publishing hundreds of books per year. Help us decide what titles to publish by submitting your suggestions to suggest@toExcel.com.

toExcel
165 West 95th Street, Suite B-N
New York, NY 10025
www.toExcel.com
Phone: 212-663-6856
Fax: 212-866-4629
info@toExcel.com